An Introduction to Business

Learning business concepts through a simulation experience

4th Edition

Accompanying the Foundation™ simulation

Dave Dusseau
Doug Wilson
University of Oregon
Lundquist College of Business

This material was developed by:
David Dusseau, Ph.D.
Doug Wilson, MBA
University of Oregon
Lundquist College of Business
Eugene, Oregon 97403-1208
541-346-3293
douglw@uoregon.edu

Foundation™ is a trademark of Management Simulations, Inc.™ and was developed by:
Management Simulations, Inc.
540 Frontage Road, Suite 3270
Northfield, Illinois 60039
847-501-2888
www.capsim.com

First published in the United States of America in 2008 by University Readers

Printed in the United States of America
12 11 10 09 08 1 2 3 4 5

ISBN (paper): 978-1-934269-21-3

Cover design: Monica Hui Hekman

University Readers
800.200.3908 | www.universityreaders.com

Table of Contents

Prologue

Most people's jobs relate to business. No matter what their major, what area their degree, or what career they choose, most will find themselves working in some type of business setting. Artists have to sell their work, physicians may work for hospitals and clinics, architects have to manage their firms and employees, and even nonprofit organizations have to pay their expenses—it all relates back to business.

This information provides a framework for understanding the essential aspects of business. The material will demonstrate how the private enterprise system and businesses that participate in that system provide value for customers, clients, and society through the products and services they offer.

The material presents an overview of business concepts by presenting information about business in conjunction with an online simulation. This simulation places *you* in the position of making business decisions for *your* company. A series of decisions you will make will enable you to see the outcome of your business choices in a competitive marketplace. The simulation requires you to establish your strategy, position your product, determine how you will promote your product, create a sales forecast, set inventory levels, and make a variety of other decisions regarding issues that most businesses need to consider.

The objective is to offer an interesting, interactive experience and to teach you about business, its terminology, and its concepts. The combination of the material you will be exploring along with the simulation will help you to better understand and appreciate the role business plays in our economic system, our society, and our lives.

Chapter **1**

Private Enterprise: An Economic System

The private enterprise system seeks to find and create opportunity through individuals acting in their own self-interest as they direct resources and compete to create and keep their profits.

Key terms to look for:

- Demand
- Economic costs
- Economics
- Innovation
- Markets
- Opportunity costs
- Specialization
- Supply

Resources are required to produce the goods and services that we need to survive and thrive in our environment. In the most basic sense, there are three kinds of resources required to produce these goods and services. These are called the factors of production and include three essential elements:

1. Raw materials *or natural resources;*
2. Tools and machinery *or capital*, and;
3. Labor *or human resources.*

Our desire for goods and services is based on our wants. In many cases, those wants are greater than the resources available to satisfy them. This scarcity of resources requires that we make choices as to how these resources are to be used.

Dictionary.com defines the term ***economics*** as:

> "A social science that deals with the production, distribution, and consumption of goods and services and with the theory and management of economies or economic systems."

Therefore, economics is a study of distributing resources for the production of goods and services within a social system. All economic systems address the same basic set of questions:

- What goods and services and how much of each will be produced?
- How will the goods and services be produced?
- Who will produce them and with what resources?
- How will the goods and services be distributed?

Communism, socialism, and capitalism are different ways in which the economic system can be structured and organized. In a capitalist, or ***private enterprise system***, individual citizens own and operate the majority of businesses and the market determines the distribution of resources. Individuals act in their own self-interest and compete to participate in transactions in the markets available to them. The terms of the transaction, or the quantity traded and the trading price is determined by the supply of and demand for that particular good.

> ***Demand*** is the quantity of goods and services consumers are willing to buy at different prices.
>
> ***Supply*** is the quantity of goods and services businesses are willing to provide at those prices.

Self-interest and competition will produce an efficient allocation of resources. Goods and services are desired and used where they produce the greatest benefit or are most productively used. Throughout this process, pressure is exerted from several areas. For example, there is pressure to lower prices and pressure to innovate through technological and procedural improvements.

This system requires the existence of four conditions:

1. Private property;
2. Freedom of choice;
3. The right to keep profits, and;
4. An environment where fair competition can occur.

There are times when this system requires boundaries. Therefore, governments establish the economic system through the rule of law and acts to correct failures of the system.

> **Back in the U.S.S.R.**
> "We want a *voluntary* union of nations—a union which precludes any coercion of one nation by another—a union founded on complete confidence, on a clear recognition of brotherly unity, on absolutely voluntary consent." V.I. Lenin's words expressed the concept behind what became known as the Union of Soviet Socialist Republics (U.S.S.R). The economic implications of this system evolved into a government that would determine what, how, and at what volume most goods and services would be produced and distributed. As if falling under its own weight, the former superpower and Communist totalitarian state collapsed in December of 1991. After surviving for more than 70 years, the economic system of the U.S.S.R. failed.

Markets

The historical creation of markets involved actual market places where potential buyers and sellers came to exchange goods and services. Today, we consider markets as any mechanism that facilitates the exchange of goods and services between buyers and sellers. The grocery store is a market where food is purchased, NASDAQ is an electronic market where buyers and sellers of stock come in contact, and the Internet enables online stores and trading sites to function. From a village square to eBay, markets have come a long way.

Markets are both specialized and complex. Consider all of the separate activities that have to be precisely coordinated in order for you to buy breakfast at a local café. Farmers, truck drivers, grocery workers, warehouses, distribution centers, cooks, and waiters represent just a few of the functions and people whose efforts contributed to the production, processing, transportation, and distribution of your meal.

In an economic context, ***specialization*** is a measure of how broadly or narrowly defined the range of included activities are. A bicycle shop is a more specialized retail store than Wal-Mart because the bicycle shop focuses on a narrow and deep range of products. Specialization creates an opportunity for greater efficiency and increased productivity. The division of tasks that comes with specialization introduces a need for coordination of those specialized tasks. These different levels of specialization and different kinds of coordinating mechanisms create a complex economic environment.

Markets are also characterized by ***uncertainty*** and ***risk***. Uncertainty is not knowing what will happen—the unpredictability about the consequences of your choice—in a decision situation. The greater the uncertainty, the less you know about the results of a particular choice. Decision makers work to reduce uncertainty by compiling as much relevant information as possible about a decision situation. Risk is also associated with the consequences of choice and, therefore, risk is a measure of the significance of those decisions.

For Example:

> Consider flipping a coin. You cannot consistently predict when you flip a nickel whether it will land with the "head" or the "tail" side up. Not knowing which side will land facing up is a form of uncertainty. If you place a bet with a friend about which side will land facing up, the amount of the bet would be a measure of the risk. If you are of average wealth in the United States and bet a nickel, then the risk associated with the bet would be small. If you are in the same economic position and bet $100,000, the risk associated with the bet becomes larger.

Decision Making

The process of defining problems and opportunities that merit attention, generating and evaluating alternative courses of action, and committing to the action that is most likely to produce the optimal result is one way to describe decision making. Decision making involves comparing the economic and opportunity rewards (benefits) and sacrifices (costs) involved in a course of action and committing to the one that best meets your goals. The objective is to make the parties involved "better off" than they were before the transaction took place. Typically, good decisions are commitments that help you accomplish your goals in whatever way you define those goals. Business decisions primarily focus on gaining economic rewards. This refers back to the assumption that we only engage in transactions that offer the potential to improve our "position." When we choose a course of action, it requires a sacrifice to obtain the reward. In economic terms, this sacrifice is a "cost." A decision maker considers two kinds of costs, the economic cost and the opportunity cost, when evaluating alternative choices available:

> The ***economic cost*** is the money spent implementing the decision.
>
> The ***opportunity cost*** is the cost of what you gave up doing when you committed to the course of action you chose.

Opportunity Cost

Assessing opportunity costs is important to determine the *true cost* of any decision. Opportunity cost can measure *anything* that is of value. The opportunity cost is not the *sum* of the available alternatives, but rather the benefit of the best *single* alternative. If there is no explicit accounting or monetary cost attached to a course of action, ignoring opportunity costs may create an illusion that the derived benefits cost nothing at all and therefore become a ***hidden cost*** associated with that action. The opportunity cost of a business decision to build a new plant facility on a business's vacant land, for example, is the loss of the land for another purpose, such as use as a parking lot, *or* to build a facility to be leased to another business, *or* to have access to the cash that could have been generated from selling the land. Only one choice is possible. Only one benefit is attainable.

For example:

Consider the decision you made after graduating from high school. You had only two choices:

1. You could have begun working immediately after high school and taken a job that pays $24,000 a year
2. You could attend a college or university with the goal of earning a degree.

The *economic cost* of the college alternative is the cost of tuition, books, fees, and living expenses while you attend school. The *opportunity cost* of the college alternative is the income that you gave up when you did *not* take the job. In the long run, opportunity costs are often more important than economic costs.

Business decisions consider economic and opportunity costs and provide a structure to make those decisions. Business has its own vocabulary and there are terms that will be helpful to know. A few of these terms include the following:

- A ***business*** is an organization or individual that seeks a profit by providing products that satisfy people's needs (or wants).
- A ***product*** is a good, service, or idea that has both tangible and intangible characteristics that provide the satisfaction or benefits.
- ***Profit***, the basic goal of business, is the difference between what it costs to make and sell a product and what the customer pays for it.
- ***Stakeholders*** are groups of people who have a vested interest ("stake") in the actions a business takes (decisions a business makes). There are four major groups of stakeholders: (1) its owners, (2) employees, (3) customers, and (4) citizens. The specific interests of each of these stakeholder groups may conflict.

Activities of Business

The most basic way to categorize the activities of business is to place them into the one of the following areas: marketing, production, finance, or accounting.

- ***Marketing*** refers to the activities designed to provide goods and services that satisfy customers. These activities include market research, development of products, pricing, promotion, and distribution.
- ***Accounting*** refers to the process that tracks, summarizes, and analyzes a firm's financial position.
- ***Production*** refers to the activities and processes used in making products. The activities involve designing the production process (investments in facilities and equipment) and the efficient management and operation of those processes.
- ***Finance*** refers to the activities concerned with funding a business and using resources effectively.

PrepMe *A business profile*

Receiving a perfect score on the SAT may have given Joseph Jewell additional confidence to pursue his business idea. At the age of 24, Jewell not only wrote a business plan and won $20,000 in the University of Chicago business plan competition but also launched the online SAT-preparation service PrepMe. With intense competition from larger companies, PrepMe is experiencing impressive growth by offering students a customized approach to study for the SAT exam. In addition to the online experience, PrepMe also offers live coaching for writing essays via email, instant messaging, and telephone communication.[1] Learn more about PrepMe at www.prepme.com.

Managing a Business

Decisions that shape the marketing, production, and financial functions of a business are often made in market environments that are specialized, complex, uncertain, and risky. Managing these functions requires planning, organizing, operating, and controlling the various aspects of the business.

- ***Planning:*** Determining what the organization needs to do and how to get it done.
- ***Organizing:*** Arranging the organizations resources and activities in such a way as to make it possible to accomplish the plan.
- ***Operating:*** Enacting the plan, including guiding and motivating employees to work toward accomplishing the necessary tasks.
- ***Controlling:*** Measuring performance, comparing performance to expectations established in the planning process, and adjusting either the performance or the plan.

In achieving the goals of the organization, managers need to be both ***effective*** and ***efficient***.

Effective *means doing the right thing.*

Efficient *means doing things right.*

Being effective involves committing to a course of action that will allow you to accomplish your goals. It is a measure of the "goodness" of the outcomes of your actions. Being efficient refers to employing an appropriate process to achieve your goals. Measures of efficiency involve comparing the resources invested to the outcomes achieved.

[1] Maggie Overfelt, "Start-ups on fire: PrepMe," *FSB*, November 2005, pp. 34-36.

Foundation™

The Web-based simulation that you will experience called "Foundation" will require you to apply these important business concepts. You will address marketing, production, accounting and finance issues as you take over your company's production and sale of goods. You will need to plan, organize, operate, and control the direction of your company as you compete for market share with other firms in this free enterprise environment. With less than perfect information, you must decide what volume of product to produce, how to promote your products, how much to invest in your sales force, how to finance your expenses, and how to assess your financial performance. After each set of decisions, you will then receive your results based upon your ongoing performance in the market, the profitability of your firm, and the value you have provided your stockholders.

Foundation™ is a registered trademark of Management Simulations, Inc.

Competing in a private enterprise environment offers value for consumers. It offers customers additional choices as businesses are motivated to innovate often through technological advancements to improve their offerings and make them more attractive. It is through ***innovation*** motivation to price their products and services attractively that businesses position themselves for future success.

Review and Discussion Questions

1. What set of questions do all economic systems address and why are those areas important?

2. Define the terms supply and demand.

3. The private enterprise system requires the existence of four conditions. What are those conditions?

4. What are the general activities of business and what roles do they play?

5. What best describes the concept of "scarcity?"

6. What does it mean to describe markets as "specialized"?

7. Provide examples of "opportunity costs" that are relevant to taking this course.

8. In the long run, opportunity costs are often more important than economic costs. Do you agree with that statement? Why or why not?

9. What roles does innovation play in the private enterprise system? What is the incentive to innovate, and why might that incentive not exist in other economic systems?

10. Give an example of "uncertainty" and how it relates to risk and decision making.

Chapter **2**

Business Ethics

Business ethics involve the moral and behavioral standards people apply as they make business decisions, solve business problems, and interact with stakeholders.

Key terms to look for:

- Code of conduct violation
- Conflict of interest
- Ethicism
- Ethics officers
- Falsification of records
- Sarbanes-Oxley Act
- Social contracts theory
- Whistleblowers

The free enterprise system relies on people and companies making business decisions that are ethical. Business ethics involve more than just obeying laws and regulations. They address behavior and decisions based on honesty, fair competition, and respect for the interests of not only the company, its owners, and its employees but also the entire society. When Warren Buffet—the world's most successful business investor— was asked what he looked for in a new employee, he replied: "I look for three things. The first is personal integrity, the second is intelligence, and the third is high energy level. But it you don't have the first, the second two don't matter."[2]

Ethical organizations practice the following types of behaviors:

- Treating employees, customers, investors and the public "fairly"
- Making "fairness" a top priority
- Holding every member personally accountable for his or her actions
- Communicating core values and principles to all members
- Demanding and rewarding integrity from all members in all situations.[3]

What does "fair" mean? Business ethics attempt to answer this question.

Business ethics is the application of ethical behavior in a business context. Business ethics can be examined from various perspectives, including the perspective of the employee, the commercial enterprise, and society as a whole. In the course of business, situations arise in which there is conflict between one or more of the parties when satisfying the interest of one party is a detriment to the other. For example, a particular outcome might be good for the employee, whereas, it would be bad for the company. From this vantage point, ethicists see the principal role of ethics as the harmonization and reconciliation of these types of conflicting interests.

Ethical dilemmas may occur in the following situations:

- **Code of conduct violation** — Acting in a way that is inconsistent with the organization's ethical standards
- **Conflict of interest** — Choosing actions that promote your personal interest at the cost of others
- **Falsification of records** — Falsifying records to present a inaccurate set of information to managers, owners and/or potential investors
- **Whistleblower situations** — Informing superiors or authorities of illegal or unethical organizational behavior.

Ethical Issues and Approaches

Philosophers and others disagree about the purpose of business in society. Some, including economist Milton Friedman, suggest that the principal role of business is to maximize returns to its owners. Under this view, only those activities that increase profitability and shareholder value should be encouraged. Therefore, companies that are likely to survive in a competitive marketplace are those that place profit maximization above everything else. However, others point out that self interest would still require a business to obey the law and adhere to basic moral

---

[2] Quoted by Adrian Gostick and Dana Telford, The Integrity Advantage," Gibbs Smith, 2003, p. 3-4.

[3] Alan Axelrod, *My First Book of Business Ethics*, Quirk Books, 2007, p. 7.

rules. The consequences of failing to do so could prove to be very costly in terms of fines, loss of licensure, or the company's reputation.

Another perspective is that a business has moral duties that extend beyond serving the interests of its owners or stockholders. These duties consist of more than simply obeying the law. Those that support this view believe that a business has moral responsibilities towards the so-called **stakeholders** as in, the people who have an interest in the conduct of the business such as employees, customers, vendors, the local community, or even society as a whole.

Theorists have adapted a social contract theory to business. In these situations, companies become quasi-democratic associations, and employees and other stakeholders are given voice over a company's operations. This approach has become especially popular through the revival of contract theory in political philosophy largely due to John Rawls' book *A Theory of Justice* and the advent of the consensus-oriented approach to solving business problems. This was an aspect of the "quality movement" that emerged in the 1980s.

Social Contracts Theory

Professors Thomas Donaldson and Thomas Dunfee proposed what they call ***Integrative Social Theory***, which is a version of the contract theory for business. Donaldson and Dunfee suggest that conflicting interests are best resolved by formulating a "fair agreement" between the parties by using a combination of:

1) Macro-principles that all rational people would agree upon as universal principles, and;

2) Micro-principles formulated by actual agreements among the interested parties.[4]

Critics say the proponents of contract theories miss a central point, namely, that a business is someone's property and not a mini-state or a means of distributing social justice.

Ethical issues can occur when companies must comply with multiple and sometimes conflicting legal or cultural standards. This may occur when multinational companies operate in countries with varying practices. For example, should a company be obligated to obey the laws of its home country, or should it follow the less stringent laws of the developing country in which it does business? Although in some parts of the world, bribery is a customary and accepted way to dong business, U.S. law forbids companies from paying bribes domestically and overseas. Similar ethical issues occur with regard to child labor, employee safety, work hours, wages, discrimination, and environmental protection laws.

Concerns regarding the stockholder theory of business arise from the fear that those that survive in a competitive business environment are businesses that recognize that their only role is to maximize profits, not to behave ethically. This perspective suggests that the competitive system fosters a downward ethical spiral.

Corporate Ethics Policies

Many companies have formulated internal policies pertaining to the ethical conduct of employees as part of more comprehensive compliance and ethics programs. These policies can be simple

[4] Thomas Donaldson and Thomas Dunfee, *Ties the Bind: A Social Contracts Approach to Business Ethics*, Harvard Business School Press, 1999, p. 5.

exhortations in broad, highly-generalized language (typically called a corporate ethics statement), or they can be more detailed policies, containing specific behavioral requirements (typically called corporate ethics codes.) These policies attempt to identify the company's expectations of workers and to offer guidance on handling some of the more common ethical problems. The objective of these policies is to create greater ethical awareness and a more consistent application to avoid ethical disasters.

An increasing number of companies require employees to attend training sessions regarding business conduct. The content of these seminars often includes a discussion of the company's policies along with a discussion of specific case studies and legal requirements. For example, some companies require their employees to sign agreements stating that they will abide by the company's rules of conduct. Many organizations are currently assessing the environmental factors that can lead employees to engage in unethical conduct. Others have redefined their core values in the light of ethical considerations, for example, BP's "beyond petroleum" environmental spin away from their original name, British Petroleum.

Baxter *A business profile*

Harry M. Jansen Kraemer, Jr. is chairman and CEO of Baxter, a global medical equipment and supplies company. He was shocked when he discovered that several kidney dialysis patients in Spain mysteriously died and it was linked to their equipment. Several days later, additional deaths occurred in Croatia. A team of Baxter experts determined that a fluid manufactured by another company and used by Baxter's equipment was causing a pulmonary embolism. Kraemer and this management team had three choices: hide the findings, blame others, or take responsibility. The company publicly apologized, halted manufacturing the products, shut down the plants that made the filters, and made financial settlements with all of the families affected. It cost the company $189 million. Kraemer recommended to the board of directors that his bonus should be reduced by 40 percent and other executives' bonuses should be reduced by 20 percent. "We try to do the right thing," Kraemer says. "If we live the lives we profess, we'll add shareholder value." [5] Learn more about Baxter at www.baxter.com.

Inconsistent Views

Not everyone supports corporate policies that govern ethical conduct. Some claim that ethical problems should depend on employees to use their own judgment. Others believe that corporate ethics policies are primarily rooted in utilitarian concerns and that they are mainly to limit the company's legal liability, or gain public favor by giving the appearance of being a good corporate citizen. Ideally, the company can avoid a lawsuit because its employees will follow the rules. If a lawsuit occurs, the company can claim that the problems would not have arisen if the employee had only followed the code properly.

[5] Michael Sisk, "Do the Right Thing," Harvard Business School: Working Knowledge, September 29, 2003, http://hbsworkingknowledge.hbs.edu/item.jhtml?id 3689&tmoral leadership.

There may be a disconnection between the company's code of ethics and the company's actual practices. To be successful, most ethicists suggest that an ethics policy should be:

- Given the unequivocal support of top management, by both word and example.
- Explained in writing and orally, with periodic reinforcement.
- Made doable—something employees can both understand and perform.
- Monitored by top management, with routine inspections for compliance and improvement.
- Backed up by clearly stated consequences in the case of disobedience.
- Observed as neutral and free of biases.

Sarbanes-Oxley Act

The Sarbanes-Oxley Act of 2002 was signed into U.S. law on July 30, 2002 in response to a number of major corporate and accounting scandals. These scandals including Enron, Tyco International, Peregrine Systems and WorldCom, resulted in a decline of public trust in accounting and reporting practices. The legislation is wide-ranging and establishes new or enhanced standards for all U.S. public company boards, management, and public accounting firms. Supporters of these reforms believe that the legislation was necessary and useful while critics believe it does more economic damage than it prevents. The Sarbanes-Oxley Act is also known as the Public Company Accounting Reform and Investor Protection Act of 2002 and is commonly called SOX or Sarbox.

Tyco *A business profile*

The former CEO of Tyco International Ltd., Dennis Kozlowski and its former chief of finance Mark Swartz were sentenced to up to 25 years in prison in a case that exposed the executives' extravagant personal lifestyles using company funds. They arranged for the corporation to pay for a toga birthday party on a Mediterranean island for Kozlowski's wife that was worth $2 million and for a Manhattan apartment worth $18 million that included a $6,000 shower curtain. Kozlowski and Swartz were also accused of giving themselves more than $150 million in illegal bonuses, forgiving loans to themselves, and manipulating the company's stock price. After a four-month trial, the jury deliberated for 11 days before returning 22 guilty verdicts on counts of grand larceny, falsifying business records, securities fraud, and conspiracy.[6] Learn more about Tyco at www.tyco.com.

Ethics Officers

Ethics officers, sometimes called "compliance" or "business conduct officers," have been appointed formally by organizations since the mid-1980s. One of the catalysts for the creation of this new role was a series of fraud, corruption and abuse scandals that afflicted the U.S. defense industry at that time. In 1991, the Ethics & Compliance Officer Association (ECOA)—originally the Ethics Officer Association (EOA)—was founded at the Center for Business Ethics at Bentley College, Waltham, Massachusetts as a professional association for those responsible for managing the organizations' efforts to achieve ethical best practices.

[6] Grace Wong, "Kozlowski gets up to 25 years", *CNN/Money*, September 19, 2005, http://money.cnn.com/2005/09/19/news/newsmakers/kozlowski_sentence.

Another critical factor in the decisions of companies to appoint ethics/compliance officers was the Federal Sentencing Guidelines for Organizations Act in 1991, which set standards for all organizations—large or small, commercial and non-commercial. Firms must follow these regulations to obtain a reduction in sentence if they should be convicted of a federal offense. Although intended to assist judges with sentencing, it is unclear if it has helped to establish best practices.

In the wake of numerous corporate scandals from 2001 to 2004, even small and medium-sized companies have begun to appoint ethics officers. The ethics officers are responsible for assessing the ethical implications of the company's activities, making recommendations regarding the company's ethical policies, and disseminating information to employees. They often report to the Chief Executive Officer. They are particularly interested in uncovering or preventing unethical and illegal actions. This trend is partly due to the Sarbanes-Oxley Act.

The effectiveness of the ethics officer position is unclear. If the appointment is made primarily as a reaction to legislative requirements, one might expect the impact to be minimal. Ethical business practices result from a corporate culture that consistently places value on ethical behavior starting from the very top of the organization. The mere establishment of a position to oversee ethics will most likely be insufficient. Instead, a more systematic program with consistent support from general management will be more necessary.

Professional Ethics

Professional ethics cover the myriad of practical ethical dilemmas that occur in specific functional areas of companies or in relation to recognized business professions.

Ethics of Accounting

Ethical issues regarding accounting practices address issues relating to financial reporting, trading, compensation, and payment policies and may include the following:

- "Creative" accounting, earnings management, and misleading financial analysis.
- Insider trading, securities fraud, and scams that concern criminal manipulation of the financial markets.
- Executive compensation: concerns excessive payments made to corporate CEO's.
- Bribery, kickbacks, and facilitation payments: while these may be in the (short-term) interests of the company and its shareholders, these practices may be anti-competitive or offensive to the values of society.

Ethics of Human Resource Management

The ethics of human resource management (HRM) covers those ethical issues arising around the employer-employee relationship. These involve the rights and duties owed between employer and employee and may include the following:

- Discrimination issues include discrimination on the basis of age, gender, race, religion, disabilities, weight, and attractiveness. Discrimination may also involve affirmative action and sexual harassment.
- Issues surrounding the representation of employees and the democratization of the workplace such as union busting and strike breaking.

- Issues affecting the privacy of the employee such as workplace surveillance and drug testing.
- Issues affecting the privacy of the *employer* such as whistleblowing.
- Issues relating to the fairness of the employment contract and the balance of power between employer and employee. This includes slavery, indentured servitude and other aspects of employment law.
- Occupational safety and health.

Ethics of Sales and Marketing

Marketing which goes beyond the mere provision of information about (and access to) a product may seek to manipulate values and behavior. To some extent, society regards this as acceptable, but where is the ethical line to be drawn? Marketing ethics overlap strongly with media ethics, because marketing makes heavy use of media. However, media ethics is a much larger topic and extends outside business ethics and may include the following:

- Pricing issues such as price fixing, price discrimination, and price skimming.
- Anti-competitive practices such as manipulation of loyalty and supply chains.
- Specific marketing strategies such as greenwash, bait and switch, shill, viral marketing, spam (electronic), pyramid scheme, and planned obsolescence.
- Content of advertisements such as attack ads, subliminal messages, sex in advertising, and products regarded as immoral or harmful.
- Children and marketing including marketing in schools.
- Black market and grey market activities.

Ethics of Production

This area of business ethics deals with the duties of a company to ensure that products and production processes do not cause harm. Some of the more acute dilemmas in this area arise out of the fact that there is usually a degree of danger in any product or production process, and it is either difficult to define a degree of permissibility or the degree of permissibility may depend on the changing state of preventative technologies or changing social perceptions of acceptable risk. Ethical issues relating to production may include the following:

- Defective, addictive, and inherently dangerous products and services such as tobacco, alcohol, weapons, motor vehicles, chemical manufacturing, and bungee jumping.
- Ethical relations between the company and the environment such as pollution, environmental ethics, and carbon emissions trading.
- Ethical problems arising out of new technologies such as genetically modified food, mobile phone radiation and health.
- Product testing ethics including animal rights and animal testing, use of economically disadvantaged groups (such as students) as test objects.

Ethics of Intellectual Property, Knowledge and Skills

Knowledge and skills are valuable but not easily "ownable" objects. It may not be obvious who has the greater rights to an idea: the company who trained the employee or the employee themselves? Does the country in which the plant grew, or the company that discovered and developed the plant's medicinal potential own the resource? As a result, attempts to assert ownership and ethical disputes over ownership arise. These ethical issues may include the following.

- Patent infringement, copyright infringement, and trademark infringement.
- Misuse of the intellectual property systems to stifle competition such as patent misuse, copyright misuse, patent troll, and submarine patent.
- Intellectual property itself has been criticized on ethical grounds.
- Employee raiding such as the practice of attracting key employees away from a competitor to take unfair advantage of the knowledge or skills they may possess.
- The practice of employing all of the most talented people in a specific field, regardless of need, in order to prevent any competitors from employing them.
- Biopiracy, which involves the appropriation of legal rights over indigenous biomedical knowledge without compensation to those who originally developed this knowledge
- Business intelligence and industrial espionage.

International Business Ethics

The issues here are grouped together because they involve a much wider, global view on business ethic matters. Looking back at the international developments of 1990s, international business ethics did not emerge until later in that decade. Many new practical issues arose out of the international context of business. Theoretical issues such as cultural relativity of ethical values receive more emphasis in this field. Other, older issues can be grouped here as well. Issues and subfields include:

- The search for universal values as a basis for international commercial behavior.
- Comparison of business ethical traditions in different countries.
- Comparison of business ethical traditions from various religious perspectives.
- Ethical issues arising out of international business transactions such as bioprospecting and biopiracy in the pharmaceutical industry; the fair trade movement, and transfer pricing.
- Issues such as globalization and cultural imperialism.
- Varying global standards, such as, the use of child labor.
- The way in which multinationals take advantage of international differences, such as outsourcing production (clothing) and services (call centers) to low-wage countries.
- The permissibility of international commerce with pariah states.

A Perspective

Business ethics is a form of the art of applied ethics that examines ethical rules and principles within a commercial context, the various moral or ethical problems that can arise in a business setting, and any special duties or obligations that apply to persons who are engaged in business activities. The foundation for ethical behavior goes well beyond corporate culture and the policies of any given company. It also depends greatly upon an individual's early moral training, the other institutions that affect an individual, the competitive business environment the company is in and, indeed, society as a whole. The demand for more ethical business processes and actions—known as ethicism—is increasing. Simultaneously, pressure is applied on industry to improve business ethics through new public initiatives and laws. Although companies may set ethical standards and offer guidelines, the ultimate decision on whether to abide by ethical principles rests with the individual.

Additional Resources

These links provide additional information and resources regarding business ethics issues.

- Institute of Business Ethics (IBE)
  http://www.ibe.org.uk/teaching/home.html

- Colorado State University, Business Ethics
  http://lib.colostate.edu/research/business/ethics.html

- E-Business Ethics
  http://e-businessethics.com/

- Mendoza College of Business Video Gallery
  http://www.nd.edu/~cba/011221/press/2007/videoGallery.shtml

- A link to background info on Steve Mariotti, the teacher at the Boys and Girls High School in Brooklyn
  http://stevenvanyoder.com/business-marketing/nifty-program.php

- Links for Enron case
  http://www.businessethics.ca/enron/

- The Wharton Ethics Program
  http://ethics.wharton.upenn.edu/links.htm

- This website is intended to provide teachers with ideas and resources that allow them to structure lessons relating to TVO's presentation of *The Corporation.*
  http://www.tvo.org/thecorporation/teachers.html

Review and Discussion Questions

1. What was Milton Friedman's view of the role of business in society?

2. What is a "social contract" and how might that impact the behavior of business?

3. Is it against the law for U.S. companies to offer bribes when doing business with other countries where bribery is acceptable? What are some potential ramifications to those businesses that follow the law?

4. Should corporate policies govern ethical conduct? What are some supporting and opposing views?

5. What are some attributes that "should" be incorporated into the ethics policy?

6. What is the role of an "Ethics Officer?"

7. Why is the effectiveness of ethics officers inconclusive?

8. What is an example of an ethics issue relating to the field of accounting?

9. What is an example of an ethics issue relating to the field of human resource management?

10. What is an example of an ethics issue relating to the field of sales and marketing?

11. What is an example of an ethics issue relating to the field of production?

12. What is an example of an ethics issue relating to the field of intellectual property rights?

13. What is an example of an ethics issue relating to the field of international business?

Chapter **3**

Accounting:
A Business Information System

Accounting tracks, summarizes, and reports business operations in a way to assist with performance assessment and better decision making for the future.

Key terms to look for:

- Assets
- Balance sheet
- Cash flow
- Contribution margin
- Dividend
- GAAP
- Gross margin
- Income statement
- Liabilities
- Owner's Equity
- Liquidity
- Net income
- Retained earnings

A company has a responsibility to its stakeholders—a diverse group of people with different needs from the company. This group includes:

- Owners
- Employees
- Customers
- Citizens (and the government that represents their interests)
- Creditors and financial institutions

These groups use accounting information to determine the degree to which the company is meeting its responsibilities. Accounting provides a function that helps managers monitor the operations of the business and report their financial conditions to those inside and outside of the business. Managers can assess the performance of production, marketing, and finance decisions, and they may rely on accounting information to detect inefficient use of resources. Optimizing the use of resources—time, materials, and money—may result in greater efficiency and therefore generate greater earnings.

The accounting system of a business generates information about the economic consequences of a company's activities. It is the historical summary and analysis of an organization's financial condition. These activities are identified, measured, recorded, and retained, and then communicated in a set of accounting reports, or statements. Management accounting provides vital information about a company to internal users; financial accounting gives information about a company to external users.

Management Accounting

Management accounting helps managers plan, operate, and control a company's activities. The information provided through management accounting gives people working for a company vital business information. Managers need information to help them compete in a world market in which technology and methods of production are constantly changing. Managers must manage data in a way that will let them use the data more efficiently and effectively. Accounting is one of the critical tools of information management.

The management accounting system provides information for managers inside the company. It is free from the restrictions of outside regulation and can be expressed in the form that is most useful for managers. Information can be reported in dollars, units, hours worked, products manufactured, numbers of defective products, or the quantity of contracts signed. Management accounting has to produce information that is relevant to specific segments of the company, products, tasks, plants, or activities. The sole objective for management accounting is to provide information that enables managers to make more informed and effective decisions.

Financial Accounting

Financial reports provide a source of information about the company's performance. Financial accounting involves the identification, measurement, recording, accumulation, and communication of economic information about a company for external users to apply to their decisions. External users are people and groups outside the company who need accounting information to decide whether or not to engage in some activity with the company. These users include individual investors; stockbrokers and financial analysts who offer investment assistance; consultants; bankers; suppliers; labor unions; customers; local, state, and federal governments; and governments of foreign countries in which the company does business.

Generally Accepted Accounting Principles

Over the years, a set of broad guidelines for financial accounting has evolved within the United States called the "generally accepted accounting principles," or GAAP. For these financial reports to be useful, companies must follow specific rules delineated by the GAAP. These principles have been developed to ensure that information reported is relevant, reliable, material, and valid.

The generally accepted accounting principles are the currently recognized guidelines, procedures, and practices that are used for financial accounting in the United States. These principles must be followed in the external reports of all companies that sell stock to the public and by many other companies as well. The GAAP cover such issues as how to account for inventory, buildings, income taxes, and capital stock; how to measure the results of a company's operations; and how to account for the operations of companies in specialized industries, such as banking, entertainment, and insurance industries. Many GAAP pronouncements are complex and technical in nature, and these principles do change. They are modified as business practices and decisions change as the Internal Revenue Service (IRS) makes new rulings and as better accounting techniques are developed.

Without these agreed-upon principles, external users of accounting information would not be able to understand the meaning of this information. Accounting is the language of business decision making. You can think of the GAAP as the agreed-upon rules of "spelling and grammar" for business communication. These rules provide a consistent basis for understanding and communicating about the financial aspects of business activities.

Management Activities

To help ensure the success of the company, managers use accounting information as they perform the activities of planning the operations of the company, operating the company, and controlling the operations of the company for future planning and operating decisions.

Planning

Management begins with planning. Planning establishes the company's goals and the means of achieving these goals. Managers use the planning process to identify what resources, such as technological, human, and material, that the company needs to achieve its goals. They use the planning process to set standards, or "benchmarks," against which they later can measure the company's progress toward its goals. By periodically measuring the company's progress against those standards, managers identify when and how the company needs to make adjustments. Because the business environment changes so rapidly, planning is an ongoing process and must be flexible enough to deal with change.

To be effective in the planning process, managers have to consider the characteristics of the environment external to the organization. This includes the economic system, the political climate, the relative health of the monetary system, and the strength of the markets in which they operate. Managers must also create and communicate these plans in the social context of the organization. A plan is good only if everyone believes in it. Accounting information plays an important role in capturing what has taken place in the past as a basis on which to create a compelling and measurable view of the company's future.

Operating

Operating refers to the set of activities that enable the company to conduct its business according to its plan. A company's operating activities ensure that products or services get made and sold as planned and on schedule. This involves gathering the resources and employees necessary to achieve the goals of the company, establishing organizational relationships among departments and employees, and working toward achieving the goals of the company.

In the process of operating a company, managers and work teams must make day-to-day decisions about how best to achieve these goals. For example, accounting information gives them valuable data about a product's performance. With this information, they can decide which products to continue to sell and when to add new products or drop old ones. If the company is a manufacturing company, managers and work teams can decide what products to produce and whether there is a better way to produce them. Accounting information enables managers to also make decisions about how to establish product prices, whether to advertise and how much to spend on advertising, and whether to buy new equipment or expand facilities. These decisions are ongoing. The results and outcomes of these decisions are reviewed, and that information is used to make the next set of decisions.

Controlling

Controlling is the management activity that measures actual operations against standards or benchmarks. It provides feedback for managers to correct deviations from those standards, and to plan for the company's future operations. Controlling is a continuous process that attempts to prevent, detect, and correct problems as quickly as possible.
Planning, operating, and controlling all require information. The company's accounting system provides much of the quantitative information that managers use.

Accounting Support for Management Activities

Management accounting involves the identification, measurement, recording, accumulation, and communication of economic information about a company for internal users in management decision making. Internal users include individual employees, work groups or teams, departmental supervisors, divisional and regional managers, and "top management." With the help of the management accountant, these internal users use this information to help them make more effective decisions.

The reports that result from management accounting may forecast revenues (amounts charged to customers), predict costs of planned activities, and provide a business analysis based on these forecasts. By describing how alternative actions might affect the company's profit and solvency, these forecasts and analyses help managers plan.

Managers use accounting information to make day-to-day decisions about what activities will best achieve the company's goals. Management accounting helps managers make these decisions by providing timely economic information about how each activity might affect the organization.

Accounting information also plays a vital role in helping managers control the operations of the company. Managers use the revenue and cost estimates generated during the planning and decision-making process as a benchmark and then evaluate the company's actual revenues and costs against that benchmark. The deviation between the forecasted and actual numbers has to be explained. Either the forecasting process has to be improved or operational decisions need to be adjusted.

Since managers are making decisions about their own company, the information the management accountant provides is designed to meet the specific information needs of the manager. This involves selecting the appropriate information to be reported, presenting that information in an understandable format, interpreting the information when necessary, and providing the information when it is needed for the decisions that are being made.

Management accounting varies widely from company to company and the responsibilities and activities continue to evolve in response to the need for new information brought about by the changing business environment. In response to that environment, the Institute of Management Accountants (IMA) publishes guidelines for management accounting called Statements on Management Accounting, or SMAs. The SMAs are nonbinding (they are not rules that must be followed), but management accountants turn to SMAs for help when faced with new situations.

In order to see how a company's accounting information helps managers in their planning, operating, and evaluating activities, consider the following three key management accounting reports that relate to budgets, cost analyses, and manufacturing costs.

1. Budgets
Budgeting is the process of quantifying managers' plans and showing the impact of these plans on the company's operating activities. Managers present this information in a budget (forecast). Once the planned activities have occurred, managers can evaluate the results of the operating activities against the budget to make sure that the actual operations of the various parts of the company achieved the goals established in the plans. For example, a company might report a budget showing how many units of product it plans to sell during the first three months of the year. When actual sales have been made, managers will compare the results of these sales with the budget to determine if their forecasts were "on target" and, if not, to find out why differences occurred. Budgets are powerful planning and control devices.

2. Cost Analysis
Cost analysis is the process of defining the costs of specific products or activities within a company. A manager will use a cost analysis to decide whether to stop or to continue making a specific product. The cost analysis would show that product's contribution to profitability at different levels of sales. Assigning (or defining) costs to products and activities is a complex activity. Every decision maker in the company has to be familiar with the way relevant costs are assigned in order to make appropriate decisions. Consistency in this reporting process is critical to ensure this information is accurate and has meaning.

3. Manufacturing Cost Reports
As we mentioned above, managers must monitor and evaluate a company's operations to determine whether its planned goals are being achieved. Accounting information can highlight specific "variances," or differences, from plans, indicating where corrections to operations can be made if necessary. A manufacturing cost report might show that total actual costs for a given month were greater than total budgeted costs; however, it might also show that some actual costs were greater while others were less than budgeted costs. The more detailed information will be useful for managers as they analyze why these differences occurred.

Internal and External Uses of Accounting Information

Both internal and external users need accounting information to make decisions about a company. Since external users want to see the reported results of management activities, these activities are discussed next, followed by how accounting information supports management activities and external decision making.

Presenting Accounting Information

Accounting information prepared for the external user may differ from that prepared for the internal user. Accounting information that helps external users with decisions such as whether or not to extend a bank loan to a company may be presented differently from the information a manager within the company needs. For instance, if a bank is deciding whether to make a loan, it will consider the likelihood that a company will repay the loan. Since this likelihood may depend on current and future sales of its products, the bank may want to evaluate the sales budget that managers developed as part of the planning process.

Many external users evaluate the accounting information of more than one company and need comparable information from each company. For example, a bank looks at accounting information from all of its customers who apply for loans, and it must use comparable information in order to decide to which customers to make loans. This need for comparability creates a need for guidelines or rules for companies to follow when preparing accounting information for external users. In addition, some external users may have a legitimate need for information generated for internal decision makers also.

Basic Financial Statements

Companies operate to achieve various goals. They may be interested in providing a healthy work environment for their employees, in reaching a high level of pollution control, or in making contributions to civic and social organizations and activities. However, to meet these goals, a company must first achieve its two primary objectives: earning a satisfactory profit and remaining solvent. If a company fails to meet either of these objectives, it will not be able to achieve its various goals and will not be able to survive in the long run.

Profit, commonly referred to as net income, is the difference between all the cash and credit sales of a company and its total costs, or expenses. Solvency is a company's long-term ability to pay its debts as they come due. As you will see, external users analyze the financial statements of a company to determine how well the company is achieving its two primary objectives.

Financial statements are accounting reports used to summarize and communicate financial information about a company. Financial statements are commonly recognized communication tools that enable people to assess the financial state of the organization. A company's accounting system produces three major financial statements:

1. Balance sheet
2. Income statement
3. Cash-flow statement

Each of these statements summarizes specific information that has been identified, measured, recorded, and retained during the accounting process.

Balance Sheet

A company's balance sheet summarizes its financial position on a given date. A balance sheet lists the company's assets, liabilities, and owner's equity on the given date. It is much like a snapshot or where the company's wealth is at a given point in time. The balance sheet is also called a statement of financial position.

Assets are economic resources that a company owns and that it expects will provide future benefits to the company. Anything owned by a company is an asset.

Liabilities are the company's economic obligations (debts) to its creditors, including people outside the company, such as banks and suppliers, as well as the employees within the company. Anything that is *owed* by a firm is a liability.

Owner's equity of a company is the owner's current investment in the assets of the company, which includes the owner's original contribution to the company and any earnings (net income) that the owner leaves in the company. A corporation owner's equity is called stockholder's equity.

A balance sheet is arranged into accounts. The value of the asset accounts will always equal the value of the liabilities and owners' equity accounts. This defines the basic accounting equation and is expressed as:

Assets = Liabilities + Owners' Equity

The following page shows an example of a balance sheet and its components.

Balance Sheet		
Assets		This includes the "stuff" or economic resources that the company has use of and from which it can expect to derive future economic benefit.
Current Assets		Assets that can (will be) converted to cash within the year.
	Cash	Currency readily available to the business.
	Accounts receivable	The amount your customers owe because they purchased from you on credit.
	Inventory	The value of the products (merchandise) that have been acquired for sale to customers and are still on hand.
	Total current assets	These are the assets used to operate your business---an important part of working capital.
Fixed Assets		Assets that have a long-term use or value, including land, building, and equipment.
	Property, plant and equipment	The purchase price that you paid for the land, buildings, and equipment that you use to create your products or services.
	Accumulated depreciation	How much of the value of your plant and equipment you have used up while operating your business over time.
	Total fixed assets	The net value of your property, plant, and equipment.
Total Assets		The value of all of the assets (stuff) of your business.
Liabilities and Owners' Equity		Where the money came from to get the assets. It accounts for who has claims against the assets of the company.
Liabilities		These are "loans," or debt contracts.
Current Liabilities		The loans that have to be paid back within a year.
	Accounts Payable	The amount that you owe your suppliers for materials (inventory) that you purchased on credit.
	Current debt	The loans (part of a long-term loan) to be paid back this year.
	Total current liabilities	The debt that you have to pay back within one year.
Long-term liabilities		The loans (or debt contracts) that have to be paid back at some point in the future (in more than a year's time).
Total liabilities		The amount of other people's wealth you are renting the use of, as if you were using their money on contract.
Owners' Equity		The value of the owners' investments in the company.
	Paid-in capital (common stock)	The value of what the owners "paid in" as a direct investment in the company. (in a corporation, the sale of stock)
	Retained earnings	The value of owners' profits that they choose to reinvest in the company.
	Total owners' equity	This is the owners' claim against the assets of the business—or the value of owning the business.
Total Liabilities and Owners' Equity		This will always equal Total Assets—as liabilities and owners' equity account for where the money came from to acquire the assets.

The Snapshot

The balance sheet describes an economic picture of a company at one point in time. This snapshot statement describes the "structure" and current financial condition of the company at a specific point in time. The balance sheet presents a picture of a company and allows you to:

- Compare pictures of two different companies at one point in time and describe the difference, and
- Compare pictures of the same company at different points in time and describe how it has changed.

Assets are the "stuff" you can use to create transactions. Your best business investment is to put your assets to work and keep them working. Assets include money, buildings, vehicles, equipment, and anything the business owns that has value. A related concept to assets is liquidity.

Liquidity

Liquidity refers to the ease with which an asset can be turned into something else, or which assets are the most liquid. Cash, for example, can be turned into inventory easily, while it is hard to turn a building into a fleet of trucks, so these are considered less liquid.

Businesses use the word "current" to mean "within one year."

Current Assets

Assets that can be converted to cash are called current assets or liquid assets. They include such things as cash, accounts receivable, and inventory.

Cash

There are several issues regarding cash management:

- Too little cash on hand cannot pay your bills without selling something or taking out more loans.
- Too much cash on hand means that your assets are not working for you as well as they might.

Accounts receivable

You have made sales, but instead of being paid in cash, you extend credit. It is like taking an "IOU." The issues involved with allowing someone to pay you after they have received the product or services include:

- How long does it take to collect (receivables period)?
- How much do you lose on customers who do not pay their bills?
- More accounts receivable this year than last indicates either that there is a more liberal credit policy or there are more sales.
- The greater the accounts receivable, the less cash there is on hand.

Inventory

The tangible quantity of goods and materials on hand is referred to as inventory. Inventory, in whatever form, is generally categorized into three areas:

> ***Raw materials inventory:*** When you purchase materials or component parts to create the product you make, those are raw materials inventory. For example, a candle factory purchases wax and wicks as raw materials.
>
> ***Work-in-process inventory:*** When you are in the middle of producing or assembling a product for sale at any point in time, materials and labor committed to creating that product are referred to as "work-in-process" inventory.
>
> ***Finished goods inventory:*** These are the finished products you have on hand, ready for sale.

The business of the company is to turn cash into inventory, and then, by selling the goods, to turn that inventory back into cash. You acquire materials and transform them. By turning cash into inventory, you create the opportunity to add value to a new product and sell it at a profit.

Inventory Issues

Managing the appropriate level, or range, of inventory is difficult.

- When there is ***too much inventory*** that you are unable to sell, particularly if those goods could become obsolete, then significant amounts of cash are tied up in products that may not sell for full price. If the products are not desirable, you may have to sell them at a discounted price or keep them around for a long time. This can be expensive because it ties up cash. As a result, you may lose money, and you may eventually run out of cash.
- When there is ***too little inventory,*** such as in a situation where you are out of stock, customers want your product but are unable to access it. They may forgo the purchase or, even worse, buy it from one of your competitors.

Fixed Assets

Fixed assets are things the firm owns that they will use for more than one year. They may include equipment, buildings, and vehicles. The value of the company's property, plant (factories, offices, etc.), and equipment is the investment the company has made in itself. It is the "capacity" of the company to create products or services. It is listed at its purchase price. The fact that they are "fixed" assets suggests that they do not have much liquidity; that is, they may take a while, more than one year, to sell these assets and turn them into cash.

Accumulated Depreciation

Fixed assets have a limited life. Trucks need to be replaced, buildings need repair, and equipment wears out. Depreciation is the process of recognizing that as you use your building and equipment to create products or services, the value of your fixed assets decreases. These assets are being used up or consumed. Accumulated depreciation is the total amount of value that has been used up since the initial purchase of the building and equipment.

Total Fixed Assets

Subtracting accumulated depreciation from fixed assets gives you total fixed assets, which is sometimes listed as *property, plant, and equipment.* Total fixed assets are the current "accounting" value of your property, plant, and equipment. This number represents the purchase price minus how much of it you have used up over time. This is *not* necessarily the same as the "market value" of your plant and equipment, which is the amount you would receive if you were to sell it right then. Companies with large accumulated depreciation have aging (old, out-of-date, or used-up) facilities. These fixed assets are worth much less that those that have been recently acquired.

Total Assets

At a given point in time, total assets are the total value of all of the "stuff" you own in your business. It includes both the facilities and the operations at that time. Looking at total assets is a common way of assessing how "big" or what "size" a company is.

Liabilities and Owners' Equity

The money to invest in your company's assets and activities has to come from somewhere. In fact, it can come from only two sources; an investment from the owners' investments (owners' equity) or loans (liabilities). Providing money to fund the assets of a company also gives the "providers" a claim against those assets. Owners' claims and debt claims are quite different from one another and companies develop financing strategies to manage these. Financing strategies are plans using debt or owners' investments to operate and grow the company. These strategies consider the differences between the owners' claims and debt claims, the goals of the company, and the nature of the industry in which they are competing.

Liabilities

Liabilities are a form of "debt contract." You have a contract that allows you to use someone else's wealth in exchange for some "consideration." For most debts, the consideration is an interest payment. This is the "rent" you pay to use someone else's money. A debt contract is for a specific period of time (length of the loan) and you have to return the wealth, or pay back the loan, at the end of the period. Borrowing money increases the amount of cash you have on hand but does not increase your profitability. Paying back your loans decreases the amount of cash on hand, but does not decrease your profitability.

Current Liabilities

Current liabilities are contractual obligations (debts) that you have to pay back within the year. Along with current assets, they account for the money it takes for you to operate your business for a given time. Together, current assets and current liabilities are called working capital.

Accounts Payable

Any good supplier wants you to buy from them, not from someone else. To make it easier and more attractive to buy, the supplier may offer you the use of their products or materials without payment for a certain number of days. The balance in this account is the amount that you owe to your suppliers for the materials (inventory) that you purchased on credit and have not yet paid for. This is referred to as buying on terms, and those terms specify the number of days that you have access to these products before having to pay for them. The phrase "net 30" for example, means that you do not have to pay for the products until 30 days after the day you received them. It is attractive for businesses to pay their bills as late as possible, without incurring expensive interest charges, so they can optimize their use of available cash.

Current Debt

The balance in this account is the amount of debt. This includes short-term loans, which are due in a year, or the current part of a long-term loan that needs to be paid back this year.

Total Current Liabilities
Current liabilities are the debts that you have to pay back this year. In general, it is extremely important that you have enough cash (or combination of cash and other current assets) to be able to meet your debt (contractual obligations) for the coming year.

Long-Term Liabilities
Loans, or debt contracts, that you have longer than one year to pay back. These could be the not-current part of *long-term bank loans* or *bonds*, which are loans that you take directly from the market.

Total Liabilities
This accounts for how much of other people's wealth you are using, or renting, on contract. This number represents the total amount of the company's debt. If you divide this number by total assets (or total liabilities and owners' equity) it will tell you what percentage of the assets was funded by debt. This is referred to as the "debt-to-assets ratio" and can be a valuable measurement tool for determining how your total debt compares to your total assets.

Owners' Equity
Owners' equity is a measure of the value of the owners' investments in the company. Generally, accounting systems keep track of how much the owners pay in (out of their own pockets) and how much of the wealth created in the owners' name, or profits the company creates, is reinvested in the company. The amount that owners reinvest in the company is called retained earnings.

Paid-in Capital
Paid-in capital, also referred to as common stock, is the owners' investment in the company. In a corporation, this is the money received from the sale of common stock. To increase the balance in this account, you have to sell more stock.

Retained Earnings
When a company makes a profit, it belongs to the owners of the company. Profits can be given to the owners to use in whatever way they want. An owner can decide to do one of two things with profits.

1. They can make a payment out of profits, which is called a ***dividend.***
2. They can be reinvested back into the company, which is called ***retained earnings***.

The balance in the retained earnings account is the value of the profits the owners choose to reinvest in the company. The balance in this account and all of the dividends ever paid will equal all of the profits made by the company. In both cases, these come from profits the business made.

Total Owners' Equity
This is the owners' claim against the assets of the business or the value of owning the business itself. In a corporation, if you divide owner's equity by the total number of shares, it gives you the value of the claim that each share has against the assets of the company. This is called ***book value.***

Total Liabilities and Owners' Equity
This is the value of all of the loans and investments that have been made in the company. Because it describes where the money came from to fund the assets and it describes the claims against the assets of the company, it will *always equal* the value of the total assets of the company.

Two of the accounts are so important that they require additional explanation. The income statement explains the activity in the retained earnings account. This is an owners' equity account that records revenues and expenses. The cash-flow statement explains activity in the cash account, or in an asset account.

Income Statement
A company's income statement summarizes the results of its operating activities for a specific time period—often one year—and shows the company's profit for that period. It shows a company's revenues, expenses, and net income (or net loss) for that time period. The income statement tracks revenues and expenses.

Revenues are the total of the prices charged to a company's customers for the goods or services the company provides to them.

Expenses are the costs of providing the goods or services.

Net income is the excess of revenues over expenses, or the company's profit; a net loss arises when expenses are greater than revenues.

These amounts include the costs of the products the company has sold (either the cost of making or purchasing these products), the costs of conducting business (called operating expenses), and the costs of income taxes, if any. The result impacts net income as profit or as loss.

A Simple Income Statement

Income Statement		
Revenue		Funds that come into the company from the sale of goods or services. These can be sales that are in cash or on-account.
Variable Costs		Costs that vary with the level of activity—the more products you make, the greater the total cost.
	Material costs	The cost of the materials (raw material and component parts) that are used in the products you sold.
	Labor costs	The cost of the labor (human resources) used to produce the products sold.
	Inventory carrying costs	The costs (warehousing, insurance, etc.) of having inventory available for sale but not yet sold.
	Total variable cost Cost of Goods Sold (COGS)	This is the cost of making the products sold.
Contribution Margin		The difference between the revenue brought in by sales and the cost of making the products for sale. This difference is what is left over to operate your business and as profit.
Period Costs		Those costs that are fixed over a period of time. These do not vary with the level of activity.
	Depreciation	This figure recognizes the amount of value that operating a business "uses up" in the plant (factory) and equipment.
	Research and Development (R& D)	The investment the company makes in developing new products or improving existing ones.
	Marketing expense	The investment the company makes in advertising, selling, and distributing products.
	Administrative expense	The cost of running a business; legal expenses, accounting services, etc.
	Total period costs	The costs of operating your business over a period of time
Earnings Before Interest and Taxes (EBIT), or Net Margin		Revenues minus variable costs (contribution margin) minus period costs.
	Interest expense	The rent you pay to use other people's wealth. This is the expense of your financing strategy.
	Taxes	The tribute you pay to the government as a citizen of a society.
Net Income		Revenues minus variable costs minus period costs minus interest expenses and taxes. This is synonymous with profit, earnings, "return," and "bottom line." Creating net income for its owners is the reason a business exists.

More on the Income Statement

The income statement is a description of the activity in transactions that affect the retained earnings account. These activities are the operating transactions that define the owners' change in wealth. The income statement tells a story about the activity of a company over a period of time. It describes the sales and all of the expenses and defines how much profit was created. Because it is a story of activity, these numbers can be used to measure how well you are doing and to assess the "goodness" of your decisions in the market.

> **In Foundation™**
>
> You will find the financial statements for your company, called "Andrews," in your "FastTrack" report in the Foundations.xls file under "Last Year's Reports." With each round, you will be able to acquire a tremendous amount of information, including your balance, income, and cash-flow statements based on the past year's performance. These statements will be invaluable tools to assess what impact your decisions have made and how you may make better decisions for the future. You will also be able to view pro forma statements that project what the next year may look like based on your projections.

Revenue

Revenues are the funds coming into the company from the sale of its products or services. It does not matter if the sales are for cash or credit (accounts receivable). Revenue is calculated by:

Revenue = Price (per unit) * units sold

For instance, if you sold 1,000 products at a price of $45 per unit, your revenue is $45,000.

Variable Costs

Variable costs are costs that are directly related to making the *products that you sell*. For instance, if the product you were making were electronic sensors, you would want to know how much each unit cost to make. If you add all of the variable costs together, you determine a "cost per unit." For example, if it cost $12.00 for the materials and $8.00 for the labor to transform the materials into the finished product the cost per unit is $20.00. Your total variable costs would be equal to the unit cost multiplied by the number of units sold.

$20 cost per unit x 1,000 units = $20,000 total variable costs

This is the "cost of goods sold, " or COGS. In a period of time, you might make more than you sell and would "spend" more money than is recognized as an income statement expense. An easy way to remember this is that it represents the **cost of goods sold,** <u>not</u> the cost of goods <u>produced</u>. If you divide the total variable costs by price, you get a percentage of every sales dollar (revenue) that goes into making the product. The lower the percentage of the cost of goods, the more efficient the company is at making products.

Contribution Margin

The contribution margin is shown on the income statement. The contribution margin number is determined by total revenues minus the variable costs. In the example, it would be:

\$45,000 - \$20,000 = \$25,000

The total contribution margin is \$25,000 and this can also be calculated as a per-unit number. If the price per unit is \$45 and cost per unit is \$20, the per-unit contribution margin is \$25. (If you multiply the per-unit information by the number of units sold, you get the contribution margin on the income statement.)

If you divide the contribution margin by revenue, you get a percentage of each dollar sold that remains after you pay for the cost of making the products that were sold.

\$25,000 / \$45,000 = 55.56%

— or —

\$25 per unit / \$45 per unit = 55.56%

Therefore, after the variable costs for the units sold have been paid, 55.56 cents out of every dollar of sales remains within the business.

Gross Margin

Gross margin is a related concept to contribution margin, but also recognizes depreciation expenses:

Revenue = (Variable Costs + Depreciation)

By including depreciation, gross margin includes the complete cost of making a product; the cost of material, labor, and the consumption (or using up) of the equipment. The higher the gross margin, the more efficient the company is in its production. Gross margin is often expressed as a percentage of sales.

Gross Profits / Net Sales

Period Costs

Period costs include depreciation expenses, research and development expenses, and administrative expenses.

Depreciation expenses

Depreciation expenses are expenses assigned to the consumption of the value of facilities and equipment. Depreciation is unique in that it is a non-cash expense. It does not cost anything, but it lowers both net income (profit) and taxes. Each year, this expense "accumulates" on the balance sheet.

Sales, General and Administrative Expenses (SG&A)

The category of Sales, General and Administrative Expenses, also referred to as SG&A, captures the fixed expenses associated with research and development, marketing, promotional and sales expenses, and general administrative expenses. Together, these expenses make up the ongoing costs of being in business. They are the cost of creating, developing, marketing, and selling products. These also recognize the expenses of making decisions. Managers need to gather information about their environment, about their markets and their customers, and about their operations in order to make effective decisions.

Earnings Before Interest and Taxes (EBIT)

EBIT is a measure of how profitable you are before subtracting the cost of your financing strategy; that is, your interest payments.

Interest

Interest payments are the rent you pay on your loans. Generally, the more loans you have, the more risky you are, and the higher interest rate you pay. The interest payment that you have to pay is a function of how much money you owe, how long you are borrowing it for, and the rate of interest you are paying. In general, the interest payment is the cost of your financial strategy. The interest, or "rent," you pay on a loan is an expense for having access to money and is an expected part of doing business. Interest is a business expense that reduces your profitability.

Net Income

Net income is the profit a firm creates by engaging in transactions. It is the firm's revenues minus all expenses. The net income generated by a company belongs to the owners of the company. The owners can choose to use this created wealth for personal purposes (that is, take it out of the company) or use the wealth to make the company bigger and more competitive (that is, reinvest it in the company). Because the goal of a business is to make a profit, the net income figure is used in several measures of business success:

Return on Sales - ROS: A measure of how much profit was created for every dollar of sales.

ROS = Net Income / Sales

Return on Assets - ROA: a measure of how much profit was created for the assets gathered.

ROA = Net Income / Total Assets

Return on Equity - ROE: a measure of how much profit was created with owners' investments.

ROE = Net Income / Owners' Equity

Earnings Per Share - EPS: a measure of how much profit was created for each share of stock.

EPS = Net Income / Number of shares outstanding

The Cash-Flow Statement

A company's cash-flow statement summarizes its cash receipts, cash payments, and net change in cash for a specific time period. The cash receipts and cash payments for operating activities, such as products sold or services performed and the costs of producing the products or services, are summarized in the Cash Flows from Operating Activities section of the statement.

The cash receipts and cash payments for investing activities are summarized in the cash flows. Investing activities include the purchases and sales of assets such as buildings and equipment. The cash receipts and cash payments for financing activities, such as money borrowed from and repaid to banks, are summarized in the Cash Flows from Financing Activities section of the statement.

Smith's Home Furnishings *A business profile*

This retail furniture store was in the middle of a rapid expansion program and opened several stores in a relative short period of time. It appeared that the business was thriving. Rather than paying for these new buildings, however, Smith's Home Furnishings was leasing them. They had also made arrangements with furniture manufacturers to allow the stores to have the manufacturers' inventory on the showroom floor without paying for it until it was sold. Smith's was a company that owned very few assets and had acquired a tremendous amount of debt. Due to this expansion, Smith's debt-to-assets ratio was much higher compared to acceptable industry standards, and as a result the business was forced into bankruptcy.

The cash-flow statement's unique purpose is to track the in-flow and out-flow of cash; for example, when a company spends money to produce inventory. As shown in the example below, under "Inventory" for the year 2007 in the far right column, a negative figure in the inventory line represents the value of the cash required for that expense of ($2,353). When that inventory is sold, and evidently that same amount was all sold in the year 2006, that sale generates cash and shows a positive figure of $2,353. The cash-flow statement will also be addressed in the next section along with the subject of working capital.

A Simple Cash Flow Statement

	2006	2007
Cash Flows from Operating Activities		
Net Income (Loss)	$2,382	$2,485
Adjustment for non-cash items		
Depreciation	$960	$960
Extraordinary gains/losses/write-offs	$22	$0
Change in Current Assets and Liabilities		
Accounts Payable	$339	$855
Inventory	$2,353	($2,353)
Accounts Receivable	($902)	$3,647
Net cash from operations	$5,154	$5,593
Cash Flows from Investing Activities		
Plant Improvements	$0	$0
Cash Flows from Financing Activities		
Dividends Paid	$0	($1,000)
Sales of Common Stock	$2,000	$0
Purchase of Common Stock	$0	$0
Cash from long-term debt	$0	$0
Retirement of long-term debt	($1,000)	$0
Change in current debt (net)	$0	$0
Net cash from financing activities	$1,000	($1,000)
Net Change in Cash Position	$6,154	$4,593
Closing Cash Position	$11,747	$5,593

Note: *Negative cash flows are denoted by numbers in parentheses in this example. Negative values may also be noted with a negative sign in front of the number and/or the number being shown in red.*

> **Koss Corporation** *A business profile*
>
> Michael Koss is president of Koss Corporation, a company that manufactures stereos headphones. He now knows the importance of cash flow management from experience. Koss expanded rapidly during the 1980's and it did not have sufficient cash flow. The corporation filed for reorganization under Chapter 11 and bankruptcy and emergency actions saved the business. Today, Koss manages with the determination never to repeat the same mistake. "I look at cash every single day" says Koss. "That is absolutely critical." [7] Learn more about the Koss Corporation at www.koss.com.

Annual Reports

A company may publish its income statement, balance sheet, and cash-flow statement, along with other financial accounting information, in an annual report. A company that is publicly traded, where stockholders have purchased shares of the company, is required to publish an annual report by the Securities and Exchange Commission to communicate their financial performance.

For example, you can find Disney's annual report at:

http://corporate.disney.go.com/investors/annual_reports.html

Applying the Information

The ability to be able to "read" and understand financial statements is valuable in understanding the financial status of any business that makes this information available. Once you have a basic understanding, the standardization imposed by the Generally Accepted Accounting Principles enables you to review and interpret almost any organization's financial statements, such as those presented in an annual report. This will be an important skill as you look at the financial information of a potential employer, an investment opportunity, or for your own business.

[7] Karen M. Kroll, "Cash Wears the Crown," *Industry Week*, May 6, 1996. pp. 16-18.

Review and Discussion Questions

1. The accounting system generates information regarding what?

2. Who relies on this information?

3. Cost analysis is best described as what?

4. What are some of the main benefits a well-planned budget offers?

5. What are some examples of current and long-term assets?

6. Why is it important to know what the contribution margin is on a product basis?

7. What type of information is found on the balance sheet?

8. What type of information is found on the income statement?

9. What is a common problem of inventory management?

10. Describe what depreciation represents.

11. What statement would you refer to in order to find the profit that a company made last year?

12. What statement would you review to find what you invested in advertising last year?

13. From what statement would you determine how much you paid in taxes last year?

14. Review the cash-flow statement example on page 40. Explain what might have occurred in the accounts receivable in the years 2006 and 2007.

Chapter **4**

Marketing: Concept and Application

Marketing is the process of planning and executing the conception, pricing, promotion and distribution of ideas, goods and services to create exchanges that satisfy individual and organizational objectives.

— American Marketing Association

Key terms to look for:

- Marketing mix
- Market research
- Marketing strategy
- Promotion
- Accessibility
- Sales forecasting
- Segmentation
- Target marketing

A business must be able to entice people to trade with you to be successful in a private enterprise system. Remember, individuals will only trade goods and services *if* they are going to be "better off" as a result of the transaction. The essential questions become who are those people and how can you create value for them? Marketing addresses these questions.

Marketing defines your strategy for competing in the marketplace. Managers need to understand and develop marketing programs to promote their products and services. Business success is based on the ability to build a growing body of satisfied customers. Marketing programs are built around the "marketing concept" and performance that directs managers to focus their efforts on identifying, satisfying, and following up on the customer's needs—all at a profit.

Dell Computer *A business profile*

The lobby of one of Dell Computer's corporate offices has a huge sign that says "Think customer." This captures Dell's innovative way of understanding, reaching, and serving customers. The direct-to-customer business model Dell has created allows customers to buy directly from the manufacturer and has enabled Dell to be highly responsive to meeting customer needs in a cost-effective manner. Dell takes delivery of components with the ability to build a PC within eight hours of taking the order. This just-in-time production system is combined with a service concept based on "the Dell vision" that states that a customer "must have a quality experience and must be pleased, not just satisfied." Dell offers exceptional service and delivery, from single end-users to corporate accounts such as Boeing that purchase as many as 1,000 personal computers each week. Dell has demonstrated the power of its marketing channel combined with competitive pricing and a responsive service philosophy.[8] Learn more about Dell at www.dell.com.

The Marketing Concept

The marketing concept focuses on the importance of providing customers value. Ideally, all company policies and activities should be aimed at satisfying customer needs. Realizing a profitable sales volume is better than maximizing sales volume at the cost of profitability.

To apply the marketing concept, a business must understand how to accomplish the following:

- *Market Research:* To determine the needs of its customers
- *Market Strategy:* To analyze its competitive advantages, plans, and actions
- *Target Marketing:* To select specific markets to serve
- *Market Mix:* To determine how to satisfy those needs through addressing product, price, place, promotion, and service

[8] Source: www.dell.com

Market Research

To be successful, a business must know and understand its market. Market research is the systematic gathering, recording, and analyzing of data about problems relating to marketing goods and services. Market research is simply an orderly and objective way of learning about people; specifically, the group of people who buy from you or have the highest propensity to do so.

Market research is not a perfect science. It deals with people and their constantly changing likes, dislikes, and behaviors, all potentially affected by hundreds of influences. Market research attempts to learn about markets scientifically and to gather facts and opinions in an orderly and objective way. Market research seeks to find out how things are, not how you think they are or would like them to be. Market research attempts to find out what specific products or services people want to buy, rather than focusing on what you want to sell them.

Market research is an organized way of finding objective answers to questions every business must answer to succeed. Every business owner-manager must ask:

- Who are my customers and potential customers?
- What kind of people are they?
- Where do they live?
- Can and will they buy from my business?
- Am I offering the kinds of goods or services they want at the best place, at the best time, and in the right amounts?
- Are my prices consistent with what buyers view as the product's value?
- Are my promotional programs working by creating awareness in the market place?
- Are my sales programs working to create accessibility for my product through the distribution channel?
- What do customers think of my business?
- How does the value my business offers compare with that of my competitors'?
- Are there specific reasons customers would make the decision to purchase from my business rather than from my competitors?

Reasons for Market Research

It is difficult—maybe even impossible—to sell people things that they do not want. Business managers have to view their businesses from a customer's perspective. They combine this perspective with their sense of the market that comes from experience. However, experience is not always a good thing. This experience may include a tremendous mass of information acquired at random over a number of years, and some of that information may no longer be timely or relevant to making decisions today. Some facts may be vague, misleading impressions or folk tales that may lead an organization in the wrong direction.

Market research focuses and organizes marketing information. It ensures that such information is timely. Sound market research provides what you need to:

- Reduce business risks.
- Identify problems and potential problems in your current market.
- Discover and profit from sales opportunities.
- Acquire facts about your market to develop a marketing strategy and implement action plans.
- Assist you in making better decisions and make corrections as needed.

Conducting Market Research

Many managers conduct some form of market research every day without being aware of it. In their daily managerial duties, they check returned items to see if there is a pattern of dissatisfaction. They run into one of your former customers and ask them why they have not been in lately. They look at a competitor's ad to see what that store is charging for the same products you are selling. These activities provide a framework that enables managers to objectively evaluate the meaning of the information they gather about their market.

A more formal market research process may include the following eight steps:

1. Defining the problem or opportunity
2. Assessing available information
3. Gathering additional information, if required
4. Reviewing internal records and files; interviewing employees
5. Collecting outside data (secondary and primary)
6. Organizing and interpreting data
7. Making a decision and taking action
8. Assessing the results of the action

Defining the Problem or Opportunity

Defining the problem or assessing the opportunity is the first step of the research process. This process is often overlooked, yet it is the most important step. You must be able to see beyond the symptoms of a problem to get at its cause. Seeing the problem as a sales decline is not defining a cause, it is merely listing a symptom.

You must establish an idea of the problem that includes causes that can be objectively measured and tested. Look at your list of possible causes frequently while you are gathering your facts, but do not let it get in the way of the facts. To define your problem, list every possible influence that may have caused it.

- Have your customers changed?
- Have their tastes changed?
- Have their buying habits changed?

List the possible causes of the problem. If there are areas that cannot be tracked, realize that you may not be able to objectively measure your progress toward that goal.

Assessing Available Information

Once you have formally defined your problem, assess the information that is immediately available. You may already have all the information you need to determine if your hypothesis is correct, and solutions to the problem may have become obvious in the process of defining it. Stop there. You have reached a point of diminishing returns. You will be wasting time and money if you do further marketing research and do not gain additional insight.

If you are uncertain if you need additional information, you must weigh the cost of more information against its usefulness. You are up against a dilemma similar to guessing in advance of what return you will receive on your advertising dollar. You do not know what return you will get, or even if you will get a return. The best you can do is to balance that against the cost of gathering more data to make a more informed decision.

Gathering Additional Information

Begin by "thinking cheap and staying as close to home as possible." Before considering anything elaborate, such as market surveys or field experiments, explore your own records and files. Look at sales records, complaints, receipts, and any other records that can help you better understand you where your customers live and work, what they buy, and how they buy it.

Credit records are an excellent source of information about your markets. Credit records provide information about your customers' addresses, employment, income levels, and marital status. Offering credit is a multifaceted marketing tool, although one with well-known costs and risks.

For example:

> Your customers' addresses can tell you a lot about who they are. You may be able to get insight about their life-styles by knowing their neighborhoods. Knowing how they live can give you solid hints about what they can be expected to buy. With this information you can gain additional profile information based on zip code, such as through the PRIZM system information, which combines U.S. Census data with psychographic market profile information and can be found at www.claritas.com. This initial profile information is available at no cost with additional details available for a fee.

When you have finished reviewing the available information in your records, turn to that other valuable internal source of customer information: your employees. Employees may be the best source of information about customer likes and dislikes. They hear customers' complaints about the store or service—often the ones the customers do not think are important enough to take to you as the owner-manager. Employees are aware of the items customers request that you may not stock. They can probably supply good customer profiles from their day-to-day contacts.

External Data and Secondary Research

Once you have exhausted your internal sources for information about your market, the next steps in the process are to do primary and secondary research outside. Secondary research involves going to already published surveys, books, magazines, and other resources and applying or rearranging the information in them to bear on your particular problem or potential opportunity.

For example:

> Imagine that you sell tires. You might guess that sales of new cars three years ago would have a strong effect on present retail sales of tires. To test this idea, you might compare new car sales of six years ago with replacement tire sales from three years ago.
>
> Suppose you found that new tire sales three years ago were 10 percent of the new car sales three years before that. Repeating this exercise for previous years reveals that in each case tire sales were about 10 percent of new car sales made three years before. You could then logically conclude that the total market for replacement tire sales in your area this year should be about 10 percent of new car sales in your locality three years ago.

Naturally, the more localized the figures you can find, the better. For instance, there may be a national decline in new housing starts, but if you sell new appliances in an area in which new housing is booming, you obviously would want to base your estimate of market potential on local conditions. Newspapers and local radio and television stations may be able to help you find this information.

There are many sources of secondary research material. You can find it in libraries, universities and colleges, trade and general business publications, and newspapers. Trade associations and government agencies are also rich sources of information.

Primary Research

Primary research on the outside can be as simple as asking customers or suppliers how they feel about your store or service firm or as complex as the surveys conducted by sophisticated professional marketing research firms. Primary research includes among its tools direct mail questionnaires, telephone or on-the-street surveys, experiments, panel studies, test marketing, behavior observation, and so on.

Primary research is often divided into reactive and non-reactive research. Non-reactive primary research is a way to see how real people behave in a real market situation without influencing that behavior. Reactive research, such as surveys, interviews, and questionnaires, is what most people think of when they hear the words marketing research. Reactive market research is a complex field. It is critical to ask the right questions and to avoid creating a bias in the responses. People may answer questions the way they think they are expected to answer, rather than telling you how they really feel about your product, service, or business.

Organizing and Interpreting Data

After collecting the data you must organize it into meaningful information. Go back to your definition of the problem, compare it with your findings, and prioritize and rank the data.

- What strategies are suggested?
- How can they be accomplished?
- How are they different from what I am doing now?
- What current activities should be increased?
- What current activities must I drop or decrease in order to devote adequate resources to new strategies?

Making Decisions and Taking Action

Prioritize each possible strategy from the standpoint of determining the:

- Immediate goal to be achieved;
- Cost to implement;
- Time to accomplish, and;
- Measurement of success.

If your market research, for example, suggests ten possible strategies, select two or three that appear to have the greatest impact potential or are most easily achievable and begin there. For each strategy, develop tactics, which may include:

- Staff responsibilities
- Necessary steps
- Budget allocations
- Timelines with deadlines for accomplishing strategic steps
- Progress measurements

Based on this information, make a final decision on the strategies and go to work on the tactics.

Assessing the Results of the Action

Analyze your progress measures. If adjustments are appropriate, make them. At the conclusion of the time you have allotted for accomplishing your goal, take a hard look at the results.

- Did you achieve your goal?
- Should the decision be renewed on a larger scale?

If you are disappointed in the results, determine why the plan went awry.

The Possibilities

Market research is limited only by your imagination. You can conduct a significant amount of market research at very little cost except your time and mental effort. While large companies generally have and use a wealth of available data on many business problems, smaller companies often ignore such data because they are unaware of its existence, although it may be as close as next door. Here are a few examples of techniques business owners and managers use to gather information about their customers.

> The local public, trade school, college, or university library is a prime source of inexpensive, targeted information about business topics such as competition, the law, government, society, culture, economics, and technology. Although the resources of public libraries vary widely, the library's four walls and the size of its collection do not limit its service. New information technologies have changed libraries dramatically. Many academic libraries are open to the public. A typical library includes reference and general books, periodicals, and possibly specialized collections. Several tools and services are available to help find material.

Indexes help find information in leading magazines, journals or newspapers. Among these are the Business Index, the Business Periodical Index, the Public Affairs Information Service Bulletins (PAIS), the Statistical Reference Index, the Wall Street Journal Index, and the American Statistics Index. These indexes list articles according to subject headings; they supply the title and author as well as the publication title, date and page number. Indexes are available in several formats including printed versions, optical disks, film, CD-ROMs, and on-line databases.

The Index to U.S. Government Periodicals is another source, and much of this information is accessible online. One example is information provided by the U.S. Census Bureau found at www.census.gov.

Information about industries and individual companies can also be found under Standard Industrial Classification Code (SIC) headings. SIC is a uniform coding system developed by the federal government to classify establishments according to economic activity. Codes for specific industries are listed in the Standard Industrial Classification Code Manual. Four-digit codes define specific industries, such as SIC 2653 for corrugated and solid fiber box manufacturers, or SIC 5812 for eating establishments. Most federal government economic data and many business and industrial directories use SIC codes.

In order to manage the marketing functions successfully, good information about the market is necessary. Frequently, a market research program can disclose problems and areas of dissatisfaction that can be easily remedied, or new products or services that could be offered successfully.

Market research should also encompass identifying trends that may affect sales and profitability levels. Population shifts, legal developments, and the local economic situation should be monitored to enable early identification of problems and opportunities. Competitor activity should also be monitored. Competitors may be entering or leaving the market, for example. It is also very useful to know what your competitors' strategies are, as such knowledge may provide competitive insight.

Marketing Strategy

Marketing strategy encompasses identifying customer groups, or target markets, that a small business can serve better than its competitors, and tailoring its product offerings, prices, distribution, promotional efforts, and services toward that particular market segment. This may be referred to as "Managing the Market Mix." Ideally, the marketing strategy should address unmet customer needs that represent adequate potential size and profitability. A good marketing strategy implies that a small business cannot be all things to all people and must analyze its market and its own capabilities. This provides a focus on a target market it can serve best, increases the effectiveness of marketing activities, and provides a better return based on the use of the marketing budget.

Target Marketing

Owners of small businesses have limited resources to spend on marketing activities. Concentrating their marketing efforts on one or a few key market segments is the basis of target marketing. The major ways to segment a market are:

Geographic segmentation : Focusing on understanding the needs of customers in a particular geographical area; for example, a neighborhood convenience store may send advertisements only to people living within one-half mile of the store.

Demographic segmentation: Focusing on the attributes of the market based upon gender, age, income, education, or other measurable factors.

Psychographic segmentation: Identifying and promoting to groups of people based on lifestyle and behaviors that are most likely to buy the product. This may be based on interests, fears, behaviors, or actions that can be categorized into groups.

Target marketing enables you to identify, access, communicate with, and sell to those that are most likely to purchase your products.

Briarcliff Bike Works *A business profile*

Lucien Orza, owner of Briarcliff Bike Works, recently decided to shift his company's focus from selling relatively inexpensive recreational bikes to targeting cycling enthusiasts with high-end bicycles that cost as much as $8,000. The cycling enthusiasts that Orza is targeting make up just five percent of the bicycle market, but their spending on bikes and accessories is far above the industry average. Orza now sells about the same number of bicycles as before, but his company's sales profit margins are 10% higher.[9] Learn more about Briarcliff Bike Works at www.briarcliffbikeworks.com.

Managing the Market Mix

There are five key marketing decision areas in a marketing program:

1. Products and Services
2. Promotion
3. Distribution
4. Pricing
5. Service

[9] Farnoosh Torabi, "Profiting by Targeting the Elite Buyer," *Money*, December 2003, p. 50.

The marketing mix is used to describe how owners and managers combine these four areas into an overall marketing program.

Products and Services : Effective product strategies for a small business may include concentrating on a narrow product line, developing a highly specialized product or service or providing a product-service package containing an unusual amount of service.

Price : Determining price levels and/or pricing policies is the major factor affecting total revenue. This includes determining the credit policy: Will you allow your customer to pay for the product *after* they receive it, or do they need to pay for it *when* they receive it? In the most general sense, higher prices mean lower volume and lower prices mean higher volume. However, small businesses can often command higher prices because of the personalized service they offer. In addition, there have been situations where higher prices are associated with higher quality, and increasing the price to a certain point, results in increased volume. Hair care products are one category where this has occurred.

Promotion : This set of marketing decisions includes leveraging the Internet, various forms of advertising, salesmanship, and other promotional activities. Offering special financing or extended terms is another form of promotion. In general, effective promotional strategies are a must for businesses because of the cost of extensive advertising campaigns and the limitations such cost imposes.

Place or Distribution Channel : The manufacturer and wholesaler must decide how to distribute their products. Working through established distributors or manufacturers' agents generally is most feasible for small manufacturers. Small retailers should consider cost and traffic flow as two major factors in location site selection, especially since advertising and rent can be reciprocal. In other words, low-cost, low-traffic location means you must spend more on advertising to build traffic. Investing efforts to increase ***accessibility*** is a key factor in product distribution.

Service : This area is a relatively recent addition to the traditional four Ps —product, price, place and promotion—of the marketing mix. Customer service is another way that an organization can provide value and differentiate itself from others that offer similar or identical products. Organizations like Nordstrom, Lexus, Eddie Bauer, and the Pacific Northwest's Les Schwab Tires have created highly successful businesses based on offering exceptional customer service.

The nature of the product or service also is important in location decisions. If purchases are made largely on an impulse basis, such as flavored popcorn, high traffic and visibility are critical. On the other hand, location is less a concern for more specialized products or services that customers are willing to go out of their way to find. The ability afforded by the Internet to reach highly segmented customers online has enabled many businesses to operate anywhere and serve local, national, and international markets.

The Sales Forecast

Another aspect of marketing is to create a sales forecast to attempt to predict your unit sales and revenue performance. The sales forecast process often begins by assessing how the total market will perform. From there, you may attempt to assess your performance and what market share it will realize from that total forecast. To do this requires that you speculate on how your competitors will perform as well.

Forecasting sales is often a challenging task due to the multiple variables involved in the process:

- What will the overall economic climate be like?
- Will consumers make decisions on the same basis they have in the past?
- At what level will our competitors perform?
- Will they introduce new products, and if so, when would that be expected?
- Will there be new competitors, or will existing competitors drop out of the market?

These are challenging questions. Considering their potential outcomes may provide insight into making better sales forecasting decisions.

> **In Foundation™**
>
> You will have the opportunity to determine how much you spend on marketing and to observe its impact on your business. You will learn about the "low tech" and "high tech" target markets, their preferences, the reasons they are most likely to buy your products, and how those preferences change from year to year. A perceptual map will help you visualize how those preferences shift and progress in relation to your product's attributes. "Promotions" expenditures will impact the awareness your markets have about your product: Does your target market know you exist? "Sales" expenditures will impact the distribution and availability of your product: Does your target market have access to those products? You will also be able to compete based on the payment schedule you offer your customers. For example, your products may be more attractive if you allow your customers to pay in 60 days rather than in a 30-day time period. A part of the process will be to create a sales forecast. The sales forecast may be one of the most challenging and frustrating tasks of all as you attempt to predict your performance and anticipate how your competitors will impact your market share.

Marketing Performance

After marketing program decisions are made, owners and managers need to evaluate the result of their decisions. Standards of performance need to be set up so results can be evaluated against them. Sound data on industry norms and past performance provide the basis for comparisons against present performance. Owners and managers should audit their company's performance on a periodic basis, at least quarterly.

The key questions to determine marketing performance include:

- Is the company doing all it can to be customer-oriented?
- Do the employees make sure the customer's needs are truly satisfied and leave them with the feeling that they would enjoy coming back?
- Is it easy for the customer to find what he or she wants and at a competitive price?

In Foundation™

Your marketing strategy will determine the price and the attributes of your products. This includes your product's performance, size, and reliability. You also have access to market research conducted on each of your target markets. This research is valuable to enable you to understand what is important to your customers. You will know the range of what they are willing to pay for your products and how they want that product to perform. You also have to consider what products your competitors are offering: their prices and how their performance, size, and reliability compare with yours. Your product awareness and accessibility are other factors that influence your sales volume. Your marketing strategy, shaped by how well you understand your potential customers, will play a significant role in how successful you are in accomplishing your business objectives.

Review and Discussion Questions

1. Define the term "market."
2. What is the primary function of the research and development department?
3. Give no less than four examples of forms of distribution.
4. What is the essential goal of market research?
5. What are the differences between awareness and accessibility?
6. What elements are involved in the marketing mix and how do they interact with each other?
7. What do perceptual maps offer that other data presentations may not?
8. What does distribution mean?
9. How has the Internet changed distribution and what markets or types of industries have been impacted the most by this change?
10. What makes up a good marketing strategy?
11. Why is it important to track the impact of a promotional and sales budget and what can be learned from tracking this data over time?

Chapter 5

Production: Improving Productivity and Performance

Production involves the efficient management of resources, including people and equipment, to successfully produce and provide quality products and services.

Key terms to look for:

- Benchmarking
- Capacity
- Carrying costs
- Economies of scale
- Human resources
- Materials requirement planning
- PERT chart
- Quality control
- Raw materials
- Supply chain management
- Total quality management
- Work-in-process inventories

Production is the process by which a company produces finished goods and services. This act of making products that will be traded or sold commercially is based on decisions about what goods to produce, how to produce them, the costs to produce them, and how to optimize the mix of resource inputs used in their production. Production information can then be combined with market information (like demand) to determine the quantity of products to produce and sell at an optimal price point. This process might involve the work, ideas, and plans of the design engineers, the production manager, the plant manager, the plant superintendent, their crews, and any other department actually involved with producing the product. Production can take the form of mass production, when a large number of standard products are created in a traditional assembly line process, or it can be a more specialized process, as when individual or small quantities are created.

Therefore, production is the conversion of inputs into outputs. It is a process that uses resources—such as cash, labor and raw materials—to create a commodity attractive for a market. This can include manufacturing, storing, shipping, and packaging. Because it is a flow concept, production is measured as a "rate of output per period of time." There are three basic aspects to the production process:

1. Quantity of the commodity produced
2. Form of the good produced
3. Temporal and spatial distribution of the commodity produced

A production process can be defined as any activity that increases the similarity between the pattern of demand for goods and the quantity, form, and distribution of these goods available to the marketplace.

Production plays a key role in the objective of a manufacturing-based business to maximize profits. Profit maximization is the process by which a firm determines the price and the output level that returns the greatest profit. There are several approaches to this to accomplish this goal. The "total revenue minus total cost" method relies on the fact that profit equals revenue minus cost, and the marginal return method (marginal revenue minus marginal cost) is based on the fact that total profit in a perfectly competitive market reaches its maximum point where marginal revenue equals marginal cost.

A business needs a production process whenever it provides products or services. This involves a series of tasks where resources are used to create a product or service. This process involves planning, procuring goods to produce the products, and assigning and organizing tasks to make those products available for sale. It is important to differentiate production from operations. ***Operations*** are the functions needed to keep the company producing through a function or series of functions to carry out a plan, while ***production*** involves the actual process of creating goods and services.

Production management seeks to develop an efficient, relatively low-cost and high-quality production process of creating specific products and services. Production management can contribute to the success of both manufacturing firms and service-oriented firms. The profits and value of each firm are influenced by its production management process.

The primary resources that firms use for the production process include:

- Human resources—*employees and their skills involved in the production process*
- Raw materials—*cost of goods to create the products*
- Capacity—*production facilities, technology, machinery, and equipment*

These resources cost money. Employees need to be paid, materials have to be purchased, and building and production facilities take time and money to be ready for production. The objective is to use these resources in the most efficient manner possible. This will enable the organization to take advantage of higher production levels producing more units at a lower cost per unit.

Bang & Olufsen *A business profile*

For more than 75 years, Bang & Olufsen has created sound systems that combine cutting edge audio and entertainment technology with an emotional appeal. The challenge is to contribute to the continued growth of Bang & Olufsen by further refining and utilizing production skills that have enabled them to become one of the largest and most innovative loudspeaker manufacturers in the world. Bang & Olufsen's approach to product development and production focuses on both tradition and constant renewal. "We never forget that technology should work for people, not the other way around. We utilize only tried and tested technologies, innovatively integrated into products that offer viewing and listening experiences beyond expectations, that are a pleasure to use, and that invite you to approach, touch, and look at, even when it is turned off."[10] Learn more about Bang & Olufsen at www.bang-olufsen.com.

Economies of Scale

Economies of scale may be one of the objectives of an efficient production process. ***Economies of scale*** describes the process where the cost of each good produced decreases as the volume produced increases. This reduction in cost per unit occurs when the initial investment of capital is shared with an increasing number of units of output, and therefore, the cost of producing a good or service decreases as production increases. Variable costs (those associated with the number of goods produced) and fixed costs (costs that do not change regardless of volume) are monitored throughout this process. As output increases, fixed costs remain the same, and variable costs on a per-unit basis typically decline as production volumes increase.

[10] Source: www.bang-olufsen.com

For example:

> A company is currently in a situation with economies of scale where their initial fixed investment of $1 million is spread over 2,000 customers and their average fixed cost per unit is $500:
>
> **$1,000,000 / 2,000 = $500**
>
> If that same organization has now grown to 2,500 customers, their average fixed costs decrease as they spread these costs over a larger customer base to only $400 per unit.
>
> **$1,000,000 / 2,500 = $400**

The result is a lower unit cost. Therefore, economies of scale are particularly critical in industries with high fixed costs, also known as capital costs. A common example is a factory. With an initial fixed investment in machinery, one worker, or unit of production, begins to work on the machine to produce a certain number of goods. If a second worker is added to the production line, he or she is able to produce an additional number of goods without adding significantly to the factory's cost of operation. If the number of goods produced grows significantly faster than the plant's cost of operation, the cost of producing an additional unit is less than the unit before, and an economy of scale occurs. Economies of scale and the efficiencies this concept offers is another benefit companies seek through growth.

Scheduling

The production manager or team is responsible for producing goods or delivering services. This role is concerned with volume, production sequence, and the type of product to be produced. Three elements of management—planning, organizing, and controlling—can clearly be seen in the tasks of the production manager.

A ***master production schedule*** determines when the products will be produced and in what quantities. Dates must be met, specified quantities must be produced on time, and costs need to be controlled to make certain this process goes smoothly and meets commitments. One tool to help with this process is a ***PERT chart***. PERT stands for "program evaluation and review technique." This is a graphical representation that tracks production events with their respective time frames from start to finish. It depicts the process and maps out the time required and can identify problems in the process before even it begins.

Inventory Control

As goods are produced, they also need to be managed. Inventory control is the process of efficiently managing inventory. There needs to be enough product available for sale, but there should not be too much product unnecessarily tying up cash. An efficient inventory control system manages the costs associated with inventory.

Companies must also manage their products as they are in the process of being created. This is described as ***work-in-process inventory***, or products that are only partially completed but have required an investment of some type of resource. Products cannot be sold until they are complete, and monitoring the status of products still involved in production is important.

Another cost directly associated with inventory is carrying cost. ***Carrying costs*** are the costs of maintaining inventories. A popular method for reducing carrying costs is the just-in-time (JIT) inventory system. This system is based on having just enough inventory on hand to satisfy consumer demand. Product should always be available, but there is not an overstock of what is needed for the near future. JIT may be in conflict with economies of scale goals, however, so the organization needs to balance the use of these.

The just-in-time system is often associated with a materials requirement planning system that ensures that materials are available when needed. A ***materials requirement planning*** system or MRP helps to determine when the materials to produce the product are needed to meet production deadlines. As a firm develops a forecast for the demand for its products, it determines the time at which the materials need to arrive at the production site to meet the anticipated market demand.

The collection of partners—manufacturer, wholesaler, distributor, retailer, on-line sales site—is referred to as the supply chain. Efforts to improve the relationships among manufacturers and their suppliers are referred to as ***supply chain management (SCM),*** and its objective is to manage the connections between supply chain members in order to enhance efficiencies and reduce costs.
Supply chain management involves these five basic components:

Plan:	*The strategic plan to manage all of the resources that go into meeting customer demand for your product or service*
Source:	*The selection of the supplies that will deliver goods and services*
Make:	*The manufacturing step involving scheduling, testing, packaging and preparing for delivery*
Deliver:	*The logistics and timing of getting those products and/or services through the channel*
Return:	*The "soft" link in the chain that supports customers returning product or have had problems with the experience*

Companies such as Hewlett-Packard and Xerox, and others have developed systems that have produced dramatic results. Cisco Systems and others have developed software and Web-based programs to assist organizations as they work to realize greater efficiencies in their supply chain process.

Quality Control and Total Quality Management
Quality is the degree to which a product or service satisfies a customer's expectations. Quality relates to consumer satisfaction and is a factor regarding the firm's current and future success. Quality control is the process of testing to determine if the product or service meets the performance and other set standards of the organization before it is sold. Techniques to monitor quality may include sampling, monitoring customer/user complaints, and looking to correct deficiencies.

In some cases, quality standards are set by agencies, such as the Food and Drug Administration (FDA) and the Consumer Products Safety Council (CPSC), or by industry associations. The standards imposed by these entities affect the design, performance, durability, safety, and many other attributes of how the goods will perform and function. Quality is also used as a competitive advantage to provide "perceived excellence" compared with other consumer choices on the market.

In Foundation™

Companies are charged an inventory carrying cost of 12% of the average cost of production for unsold units remaining at year's end. Keeping inventory levels at an acceptable range—more than one unit and less than 60 days of inventory based on what was actually sold that year—will be advantageous for minimizing carrying costs. Managing inventory presents a tremendous challenge. Your production volumes will be driven by your sales forecast and therefore relate to your anticipated market share. All of these variables for each product will determine your production and resulting inventory levels.

Several techniques are used to improve quality within an organization. ***Quality circles*** are small groups of employees who meet regularly to attempt to identify and solve problems involved in quality improvement. A more formalized process is the concept of ***Total Quality Management (TQM)***.

Total Quality Management is the act of monitoring and improving the quality of products and services produced. This concept is based on the work of W. Edwards Deming and others and includes these guidelines:

To provide managers and other employees with the education and training they need to excel in their jobs

To encourage employees to take responsibility and to provide leadership

To encourage all employees to search for ways to improve the production process

Many firms create teams of employees to assess quality and offer suggestions for continuous improvement. This creates a form of cross-functional teamwork where employees with different jobs, responsibilities, and perspectives work together to improve the production process through enhanced quality.

In Foundation™

An optional Total Quality Management (TQM) initiative is integrated into the Foundation experience. TQM involves investing money in three areas: (1) Benchmarking, (2) Quality Functional Deployment Efforts, and (3) Concurrent Engineering/6 Sigma training. Investing in one or more of these TQM areas will reduce administrative overhead, carrying costs, and the research and development time-cycle while it increases the impact of promotion and sales investments. Investing the "right amount" in TQM initiatives is important. If you spend too little or too much, your returns on a per-dollar-invested basis diminish. A TQM tutorial is available at www.capsim.com that further describes this process.

Benchmarking

The process called ***benchmarking*** is another quality-improvement technique. Benchmarking describes a method of evaluating performance by comparison with another specified level achieved by another entity. Often, benchmarking involves studying highly successful companies in other industries. For example, Ford Motor Company studied and used the customer service performance levels of Eddie Bauer to improve its customer relations process. Benchmarking may also be used in conjunction with a TQM process.

> **Merritt Tool Company** *A business profile*
>
> Owner A.P. Merritt, Jr. studied Toyota's lean manufacturing process to understand how he might apply these techniques to Merritt Tool, a 65-person parts manufacturer for the aerospace industry. His team of employees began looking for a way to streamline processes to improve efficiency and minimize waste. Employees throughout Merritt Tool began to implement the new techniques and improvements were apparent. The results included a lower accident rate, higher quality, lower costs, faster delivery intervals, shorter setup times, fewer machine breakdowns, and higher employee satisfaction levels.[11] Learn more about Merritt Tool at www.merritttool.com.

Technology

Many production processes have been automated, and robotics has become a significant factor in manufacturing throughout the world. From the simple machines of olden times to the intelligent machines of today, robotics has changed the face of industry, be it from automotive manufacturing to food processing. Machines and robotic equipment reduce the labor required in the production process and although these machines may be an expense at first, their ongoing use can reduce labor expenses in time due to the efficiencies they offer. Good planning is required to make certain that the automation process accomplishes the desired goals. This involves a thorough assessment of the required costs, the savings and benefits that may be realized, and the degree of "fit" within the organization and production process.

Improving Productivity

A healthy economy often correlates with consistent improvement in productivity. A common measure of productivity is expressed in dollar of output per hour worked. Production faces the standard challenges of increasing labor, material, and opportunity costs. It also must address the impact of uncertain world events, technological change, and the global labor market. This is combined with the consumer trend of demanding higher quality standards as companies work to improve the output based on required resources.

---

[11] Mark Albert, "This Shop Really Shines …" *Modern Machine Shop*, January 2004, http://www.findarticles.com/p/articles/mi_m3101/is_8_76/ai_112862177.

In Foundation™

The production of each product takes place in a single plant. The "first shift" capacity is the number of units that can be produced on an assembly line in a single year. A second shift is capable of matching this figure while receiving overtime wages of 50% more than that of the first shift. For example, if your first shift has the capacity to produce 800 products each year, your second shift can produce that same amount for a total annual production capacity of 1,600 units. However, products produced on the second shift require overtime wages and are therefore more expensive products. But there are ways to reduce the need for overtime work. One option is automation. The production process can be automated and decrease the labor hours needed. A second option is to expand the capacity of the plant to be able to produce more products each year without requiring as much overtime (by increasing the size of the first shift). There is a one-year lag between the purchase of capacity before it is available for use. Therefore, advanced planning is required.

Review and Discussion Questions

1. Discuss the primary resources involved in the production process.

2. What does "economies of scale" mean and why is that concept relevant in the production process?

3. What might be the correlation between economies of scale and a company's growth and what type of environment might benefit most?

4. What are the key advantages of just-in-time (JIT) manufacturing?

5. Can inventory control systems, such as the JIT technique, be applied to the operation of a service-based business?

6. What benefits does TQM offer an organization?

7. What does benchmarking accomplish?

8. How does supply chain management impact the production process?

9. What are the potential benefits of effectively managing quality control?

10. What do you consider to be the single most challenging aspect of the production process?

Chapter 6

Finance: Working and Investment Capital

"Cash is king" and is the single most critical asset in managing a successful business.

Key terms to look for:

- Accounts payable
- Bonds
- Book value
- Current ratio
- Debt-to-asset ratio
- Inventory management
- Leverage
- Line of credit
- Liquidity
- Principal
- Quick or acid ratio
- Stockholder's equity
- Working capital

The activities that you engage in to run your business are kept track of in your current assets and current liabilities accounts. Collectively, these are referred to as your working capital. Cash is the most liquid current asset and is critical to running your business.

In its simplest form ...

When you operate your company, you turn cash into inventory and inventory into cash through the sales you make. However, to get the cash you need to create inventory, a company might purchase materials on account, referred to as accounts payable, or take a short-term loan from a bank. In order to generate sales, the company might sell on account to make the transaction more attractive. The working-capital cycle, also known as the cash-flow cycle, is the time between the payments of what a business owes (payables) and the collection of what a business is owed (receivables). Businesses need to manage the amount of time that funds are "tied-up" in order to reduce the amount of working capital needed for operations. This helps to make certain that there is adequate cash on hand to operate the business successfully.

Accounting Profit vs. Cash Flow

Profits, also referred to as earnings or net income, and cash flow are two different concepts. Profits are defined by accounting rules for an income statement. An accrual accounting system is where the accounting system recognizes transactions when the agreement is made, not when the cash is exchanged. This is opposed to a cash accounting system where transactions are recognized when the cash is received. Income statements also include non-cash expenses such as depreciation. When using an accrual accounting system, it is possible for a company to be very profitable and still run out of cash. This may occur when a company is in a growth stage. It is showing a profit, but does not have the cash available to pay its debts. Without cash, the company can go out of business. In addition to managing profitability, the company also has to manage its cash flow: the cash receipts and cash disbursements, or payments, over time.

Working-Capital Management

Net working capital is the difference between a business's current assets and its current liabilities. Working-capital management involves the decisions related to operating the business (working). These decisions will involve the management of cash, accounts receivable, inventories, accounts payable, and short-term bank loans.

Working-capital management is concerned with the day-to-day operations rather than with long-term business decisions. For example, plans for introducing new products to the market and plans for obtaining the facilities and equipment necessary to produce them are strategic in nature, as are the long-term financing needs of the firm. In general, long-term financing needs are best met through long-term sources of capital such as retained earnings, sale of stock, and the sale of long-term debt obligations (bonds). Working-capital management policies address short-term (issues that occur within the business year) problems and opportunities.

There is a direct relationship between sales growth and current asset levels. For example, higher sales volume may be achieved only if production increases. Higher production, however, requires more money tied up in inventory. Additionally, if a firm buys on credit, its accounts payable increase and when it sells on credit, its accounts receivable increase. Therefore, higher sales require a larger investment in current assets, which requires greater financing. Unless something is really wrong, higher sales mean higher profits. To increase profits, you have to effectively manage your working capital.

The Working-Capital Cycle

The working-capital cycle includes all the activity between the first cash spent producing a product to receiving a cash payment for its sale. The first step is when the firm orders and receives the raw material, generating an account payable. The last step in the cycle happens when you receive the money owed to you from the sale of the product on credit, which is when the account receivable is paid off.

The working-capital cycle is defined as the length of time between the payment of the payables and the collection of receivables. During this cycle, a business's funds are unavailable for other purposes. Cash has been paid for purchases but cash has not been collected from sales. Short-term financing may be needed to sustain business activities for this period. Since there is always a cost to such financing, a goal of any business should be to minimize the cycle. To achieve this goal three terms must be clearly understood:

1. ***Production cycle*** refers to the length of time between the purchase of raw materials, production of the goods or service, and the sale of the finished product.
2. ***Accounts payable lag*** is the time between the purchase of raw materials on credit and the cash payments made for the resulting accounts payable.
3. ***Accounts receivable lag*** is the time between the sale of the final product on credit and cash receipts for the accounts receivable.

Let's look at examples with different payable and receivable lags. In both examples assume it takes 40 days after an order is received to process the raw material into finished product (production cycle is 40 days).

30-Day A/P Lag: In the first example, the accounts payable lag is 30 days, and the receivables lag is 45 days. Your company receives the materials and starts to process it. Within 30 days after receiving the material, you have to pay your supplier (A/P lag); 40 days after receiving the material, you have inventory to sell. For 10 days, then, your cash is tied up in inventory that is not available for sale. If you deliver it to your customer on the fortieth day of the production cycle, your customer has 45 more days to pay for it. On that day, your cash has been tied up in inventory for 55 days (10 days before inventory was ready for sale and 45 days after).

45-Day A/P Lag—The second example has the accounts payable lag at 45 days, and the receivables lag at 30 days. Your company receives the materials and starts to process it. Within 40 days after receiving the material, you have inventory to sell. Within 45 days after receiving the material, you have to pay your supplier (A/P lag), For 5 days, you have inventory available for sale with none of your own cash tied up. If you deliver it to your customer on the 40th day of the production cycle, your customer has 30 more days to pay for it. On that day, your cash has been tied up in inventory for only 25 days. (You didn't have to pay your supplier for 5 of the 30 days after delivery).

As mentioned before, the working-capital cycle represents the time in which working capital is "tied up" in covering production costs. If a business owner is able to shorten the cycle, the need for external financing and the resulting interest expense will be smaller, thus creating higher profits.

Cash and Marketable Securities
You need cash on hand to pay your bills; for example, to pay wages, buy raw materials, and pay taxes. The question is, how much cash should you have on hand? You need to be sure you can cover your day-to-day transactions. This amount is called the transaction balance. You might want to keep some extra cash on hand to take advantage of special bargains (a supplier's clearance sale of raw materials, for example), or to take advantage of discounts offered by suppliers for early payment of your bills (accounts payable), or as a precaution against emergencies (any unexpected expense). The cash held for such purposes is called ***speculative cash balances***.

There are many advantages to having sufficient cash on hand and many problems when you do not have enough. Cash, however, does not work for you. Cash does not earn an explicit return. If you have too much cash on hand, you are not working your assets effectively and your cash is not being used in the most productive manner. As an alternative to holding large cash balances, many companies hold part of their liquid funds in short-term marketable securities. These instruments earn interest and can be very easily converted to cash. Some examples of such securities are

- ***Treasury Bills(T-Bills)*** are short-term loans to the United States government with a smallest denomination of $10,000 and that mature in less than one year. Sold at a discount, the buyer pays an amount less than the face value of the T-Bill but gets the full amount when the bill matures.

- ***Commercial Paper*** is an unsecured loan to a large corporation with good and well-established credit ratings. These loans usually mature between 15 and 45 days (but it can be anywhere from 1 to 270 days).

- ***Certificates of Deposit* (CDs)** are popular short-term instruments issued by commercial banks. CDs are issued in minimum denominations of $100,000 and may be traded in the secondary market. They are insured by the Federal Deposit Insurance Corporation (FDIC).

Accounts Receivable and Credit Management
The profitability of a business is dependent upon its ability to successfully sell its products for more than it costs to produce them. Offering to "sell on credit" attracts customers and increases sales volume. There are costs to extending credit that must be understood, however. When a company sells products without receiving cash, an account receivable (A/R) is generated. You are "loaning" your customer the money to buy your products. Normally, a loan generates some value, usually an interest payment. An account receivable "loan" usually generates value in increased sales, not in a cash interest payment. The total dollar amount of receivables is cash that is "tied up" and unavailable for other uses. This amount is determined by the volume of sales and the average length of time between a sale and receipt of the full cash payment:

Accounts Receivable = Credit sales per day x Length of collection period

For example:

> If a business has credit sales of $1,000 per day and allows 20 days for payment, it has a total of $1,000 x 20 or $20,000 invested in receivables at any given time. Any changes in the volume of sales or the length of the collection period will change the receivable position.

A credit policy refers to the decisions to grant, monitor, and collect the cash for outstanding accounts receivable. Four factors must be considered in establishing an effective credit policy: (1) credit worthiness standards (can your customers pay you back?), (2) credit period (how long they have to pay), (3) collection policy (what you will do if they do not pay), and (4) early payment discount (do you give them a discount if they pay early?).

Inventory Management

A firm's profitability depends on its ability to sell its products. A company has to have enough inventory to meet demand. How does a company know how much is "enough" inventory? They must forecast and develop sales for a period. Since sales depend on many factors outside of a business's control, inventory management is very challenging. Holding inventory levels at less than what is needed will cost the firm lost sales. On the other hand, holding inventory is expensive and involves costs such as storage and insurance expenses. Holding inventory ties up cash that cannot be used for other purposes. Excess inventory must also be avoided to maximize profits.

Typical questions in determining inventory levels include the following:

- How many units of particular products must the firm hold in stock?
- How many units must be ordered or produced at a given time?
- When should the order be placed?

As mentioned before, in determining how many units to have in stock, sales must be predicted and sufficient inventories held to satisfy the expected demand. Moreover, to prepare for potential sales increases, some level of "safety stocks" must also be held. The amount of safety stock is determined by comparing the cost of maintaining this additional inventory against potential sales losses.

The following ratios should help to determine the optimal number of each product to keep in your inventory:

- **Inventory Turnover Rate** = Cost of goods sold / Inventory
- **Inventory Turnover Days** = Number of days in a period / Inventory turnover rate
- **Ideal Inventory** = Cost of goods sold / Industry average turnover rate

For example:

> Last year your business sold goods, which cost $100,000, and your average inventory for the year was worth $10,000. The inventory turnover rate for last year was $100,000/$10,000, or 10 times. Furthermore, the business's inventory turnover days were 360 days/10, or 36 days. These numbers indicate that during the past year, your inventory turned over 10 times and, on average, it took 36 days to sell the entire inventory. When compared with industry averages, the relative strength of your business's inventory management will be revealed. A low inventory turnover rate could indicate overstocking, while high inventory turnover days can represent slow sales.

If the average industry turnover rate is 12 times, your business's ideal inventory levels for the year should have been:

$100,000 / 12 = $8,333

This figure may be used as a guideline for determining inventory levels during the current year.

Inventory Carrying Costs

Total inventory costs include the time value of capital tied up in inventories, storage and handling expenses, as well as insurance, taxes, and costs relating to obsolete inventory. These costs are generally referred to as the inventory carrying costs. Carrying costs always increase as inventory levels rise.

Short-Term Liabilities

Short-term credit is any liability with an original payment period of less than one year. Major sources of short-term credit include payables (accounts payable, wages payable, taxes payable) and short-term loans. There are both advantages and disadvantages to using short-term credit.

Speed, flexibility, and lower costs are potential advantages of short-term credit. Increased risk to the borrower is considered a disadvantage. Generally, obtaining a long-term loan requires a longer period of time because of the need for a more thorough examination of the borrower's financial statements. Short-term credit, however, usually can be obtained fairly quickly. In addition, short-term credit generally requires a lower interest rate, which is more cost effective than long-term debt.

But even though short-term debt is often less expensive than long-term debt, short-term borrowers face the possibility of paying higher interest rates as their need for new loans develops over a period of time. Over time, there also exists a potential for interest rates to increase. Consequently, short-term borrowing subjects the borrower to uncertain interest expenses as compared with borrowers of long-term funds with locked-in interest rates.

Kiss My Face *A business profile*

Bob MacLeod and Stephen Byckiewicz could not persuade a bank to lend them money for their company selling a line of natural soaps and shampoos. They pooled the $10,000 they had and invested it in the business. Sales slowly and steadily climbed as the entrepreneurs financed their company's growth with retained earnings and some debt while maintaining 100 percent ownership. Today, Kiss My Face is debt-free with annual sales of more than $30 million. [12] Learn more about Kiss My Face at www.kissmyface.com.

[12] Jenny Wonderling, "The Art of Business," Chronogram.com, April 2002, http://www.chronogram.com/issue/2002/04/business1.htm.

Accounts Payable
Purchasing equipment and raw materials represents a large portion of total operating expenses. A small manufacturing firm may spend in excess of 70% of total sales purchasing raw materials and converting them into finished goods (COGS is 70% of sales and gross margin is 30%). Accounts payable become an important source of financing in the short term. Managing prompt payments of accounts and keeping repayment cycles as short as possible make the company an attractive customer.

Short-Term Bank Loans
As a business grows, its needs for "nonspontaneous" sources of credit will grow as well. Commercial banks are major providers of short-term financing to businesses. When applying for a short-term bank loan, select a bank that best serves your needs, and then prepare for a successful loan application interview.

The provisions of a loan agreement must be clearly understood by the borrower if they are to know the true costs of the loan. Loan terms can include "hidden" costs or restrictions on business practices.

A ***line of credit*** is an informal understanding between a bank and a borrower that a specific amount of funds is available for future financing purposes. A ***revolving credit account*** is a formal line of credit offered to larger businesses in exchange for up-front fees and standard interest payments. In return, the bank has the legal obligation to fulfill its commitments under the formal agreement. Some banks require their borrowers to maintain compensating balances, which usually are a certain percentage of the loan amount. Finally, a lender can require a borrower to pledge collateral as security to ensure repayment of the loan's ***principal*** and interest.

The Banker's Decision

Factors that your banker may evaluate in considering your loan application:

1. *Your character, integrity, and overall management skills.*
2. *Your company's track record; i.e., its sales and profits.*
3. *Your product and its relative importance to the market.*
4. *Your financial statements, preferably accompanied by a certified public accountant's (CPA's) statement.*
5. *A description of the purpose of the loan.*
6. *Your company's ability to provide data to the bank both accurately and in a timely manner.*
7. *The primary and alternative sources of repayment.*

Factors that your banker may look upon <u>negatively</u> in approving your loan:

1. *Accounts receivable past due, indicating that cash is coming too slowly.*
2. *Accounts payable abnormally extended.*
3. *Poor inventory operation, such as low turnover and large back orders.*
4. *High debt-equity ratio, signifying large outstanding loans.*
5. *Large withdrawals of profits by the company's officers/owners.*
6. *Attempts to borrow short-term funds to meet long-term needs.*
7. *Insufficient financial data.*
8. *Poor credit rating for principal business owners/officers.*
9. *Personal problems of executives.*

A Financial Statement Example

You have an idea—a very good idea—about how to meet the needs of the customers who want electronic sensors. The best part is that you have a competent plan for meeting those needs and making a profit. You put together a business plan, set up a company, and meet with some people (investors) who might want to become part-owners of your company. At the end of the meetings, you have convinced 20 investors to give you $1 million each.

When you get home, you decide that you should set up a way to keep track of (or account for) the transactions you will engage in for the company. You want to keep track of both where the money came from and what you are using it for. You know that there are two ways to get money—either from the company's owners (these accounts are called owners' equity accounts) or from some form of a loan agreement (these accounts are called liability accounts). The things you have control over are called assets (and these accounts are called asset accounts). You know that these two systems will always have to account for the same amount of money because the money that you are using has to come from somewhere.

To begin, you set up two accounts: one is for cash, which is an asset you have control over, and the other is for the money given to you by the company's owners, called "paid-in capital," which is an owner's equity account. Because you are dealing with a lot of zeros, you decide to record all of the numbers without the last three zeros and you put a note stating, "all numbers in thousands (,000)." Therefore, your company has control over $20 million.

Buying Plant and Equipment

The first step in your plan is to purchase a building (a plant) to manufacture your electronic sensors. The plant and equipment cost $15 million. You arrange a loan from the bank for this purchase. The loan agreement requires you to use $5 million of your cash for a down payment and the bank will let you use $10 million for 10 years. To use the bank's money, you agree to pay them a "rent" of 10% per year (this rent is called "interest"), and to return $1 million every year.

This is a complicated agreement to account for. You have the use of a new plant full of equipment that is worth $15 million. You set up a new asset account called "Plant and Equipment" and record the purchase price in it. You know that you have $5 million less cash so you subtract that from your cash account. You also know that you owe the bank $10 million, and so you start a new account called "Long-Term Debt" and enter the amount of the loan. You do not "account for" the interest payment or the return of the $1 million until the end of each year so you ignore this information for now.

At this point, you have control of a $30-million business ($15 million in cash and $15 million in plant/equipment). Of that, $20 million came from owners' investments and $10 million from a bank loan.

In Foundation™

As you manage your company, you will be able to view and track all of the information about your company. Your balance sheet, income and cash-flow statements will give you insight about the current state of your company, its progress and its direction. This information, found in the "FastTrack" report, will help you better understand your company's past and provide information to make better decisions for its future. Challenges in predicting your sales volumes will certainly exist, but the historical information based upon this data and the information you are able to access regarding your competitors will be valuable to increase your opportunity to succeed.

Acquiring Inventory

In order to start manufacturing your electronic sensors, you have to purchase the component parts and materials. You locate the parts and materials that you believe will produce the perfect sensor according to your business plan. The businesses you purchase from are called your **suppliers** because they are the source for the materials you need.

The component parts and materials make up your inventory. You agree to give your suppliers $10 million cash in exchange for the inventory you need to begin doing business. You set up a new asset account called "Inventory" and you record the $10 million value in it. You have $10 million less cash so you subtract that amount from your "Cash" account. The total value of your assets has *not* changed (total = $30 million). You have simply changed the form of your assets—what used to be cash, now is inventory.

You are now going to begin to build a statement that reflects the impact on your cash flow. This cash-flow statement shows assets in the form of cash, inventory, and investment in plant and equipment. You also see your liabilities in the form of long-term debt and owner's equity, which is the paid-in capital, or PIC.

Assets			**Liabilities**	**Owners' Equity**
Cash	**Inv.**	**Plant/Equip.**	**LT Debt**	**PIC**
$20,000				$20,000
(5,000)		15,000	10,000	
(10,000)	10,000			
$5,000	$10,000	$15,000	$10,000	$20,000

Based on this, you are so encouraged and optimistic about introducing your new electronic sensor to the market that you revise your plan. You are willing to bet that you will be able to sell even more than you originally forecast. However, that will require $2 million more product in inventory. You know that you will need at least $5 million in cash to generate sales (for advertising and to develop your sales force) and you do *not* want to spend the cash. You contact your suppliers and discuss your dilemma with them.

Your suppliers look at your plan and at your financial records and agree that you should have no problem meeting your revised forecast. They agree to sell you additional component parts and materials, but you do not have to pay them for three months. Essentially, they are loaning you the value of the inventory for 90 days. Since loans are recorded in liability accounts, you set up a new account called "Accounts Payable" and record the value of the loan from your suppliers there. You also have an additional $2 million in inventory so you add that value into your inventory asset account. You are still in "balance," but the value of the company you control is now $32 million.

You have added some columns to your table. You expect to have current Assets and Liabilities in the form of accounts receivable and short-term debt, respectively. You also see that you are expecting to account for earnings in the "Owners' Equity" area of your cash-flow statement.

Assets				**Liabilities**			**Owners' Equity**	
Cash	**Acct. Rec.**	**Inv.**	**Plant/Equip.**	**Acct. Pay**	**ST Debt**	**LT Debt**	**PIC**	**Earnings**
$20,000							$20,000	
(5,000)			15,000			10,000		
(10,000)		10,000						
		2,000		2,000				
$5,000		$12,000	$15,000	$2,000		$10,000	$20,000	

Improving Equipment

You learn that there is a new kind of computer—it is some type of a robotic device that has been designed to work with the equipment that you have in your plant in increase productivity. You study this problem carefully weighing the benefits of having the automation versus the cost of the equipment. You decide to automate about 25% of your machines at a cost of $3 million. You take out a loan for this investment and agree to pay back the whole $3 million in the next year (and pay 10% interest on this amount). Because you have to pay back this loan so quickly (within a year), you do not want to add the amount to the loan for the original plant and equipment. You set up a new liability account called "Short-Term Debt."

You record the $3 million that you will have to pay back in the new account and you add $3 million to your plant and equipment column. The value of the company has increased by this amount to $35 million.

Now that you have set up this new account, you realize it would be more accurate to recognize the value of all of the debt that you have to pay within the coming year. That would include $1 million of the original $10-million loan to buy the plant and equipment. You account for this by reducing the Long-Term Debt account and increasing the Short-Term Debt account by that amount.

Assets **Liabilities** **Owners' Equity**

Cash	Acct. Rec.	Inv.	Plant/Equip.	Acct. Pay	ST Debt	LT Debt	PIC	Earnings
$20,000							$20,000	
(5,000)			15,000			10,000		
(10,000)		10,000						
		2,000		2,000				
			3,000		3,000			
					1,000	(1,000)		
$5,000		$12,000	$18,000	$2,000	$4,000	$9,000	$20,000	

For convenience, as you begin accounting for business operations (revenues and expenses), only the account balances (above) will be carried over in the next worksheets.

Operating Your Business

Now that you are properly positioned, you are ready to sell your product. In the first year you sell 1.5 million units at a cash price of $10.00 each. This gives you an additional $15 million in cash. When the company makes (or loses) money, this money belongs to the owners of the company. So you need to set up a new account—a new owners' equity account—for the earnings of the company. This account is called the "Retained Earnings" account. To account for the cash sales, the value of the cash account and the value of the earnings account both increase by $15 million.

The company also sold an additional 500,000 units for $10.00 each, but these units were sold on "account." This means that you are owed the money, but you do not yet have the cash. You have done this same thing where you had purchased some inventory on account (without having to pay the cash for 90 days) and you made the sale but, have not yet collected the cash. In order to keep track of this kind of transaction, you create a new asset account called "Accounts Receivable," or A/R, in which you record sales we have made but not yet received the money for. The value of sales on account is $5 million (0.5 million units times $10). The value created by this transaction belongs to the owners and so is recorded in the retained earnings account.

You sold 2 million units from inventory. Each unit has five dollars' worth of materials in it. (This is called the materials cost). To create sales of 2 million units, you reduced the value of your inventory by $10 million (2 million units times five dollars per unit). This expense is an owner's expense and is accounted for as a reduction under "Earnings."

Each of the 2 million units sold has an associated labor expense. For every unit produced, the company had to pay wages (out of cash) of two dollars. To create sales of 2 million units, it cost the company $4 million out of cash for labor. This expense is an owner's expense and is accounted for as a reduction under the "Earnings" column.

Assets				Liabilities			Owners' Equity	
Cash	Acct. Rec.	Inv.	Plant/Equip.	Acct. Pay	ST Debt	LT Debt	PIC	Earnings
$5,000		$12,000	$18,000	$2,000	$4,000	$9,000	$20,000	
15,000								15,000
	5,000							5,000
		(10,000)						(10,000)
(4,000)								(4,000)
$16,000	$5,000	$2,000	$18,000	$2,000	$4,000	$9,000	$20,000	$6,000

Unit Costs

You are selling electronic sensors for $10.00 each. To make a sensor costs you $5 for the materials and $2 for the labor to assemble it. If these are all of your costs, each sensor would contribute $3 ($10.00 price per unit minus $7.00 cost per unit) toward your profitability. This is called your per-unit contribution margin, or margin of per-unit contribution to profit.

Material costs and labor costs are variable costs because the total cost varies depending on how many you sell. For instance, if you sell 1 million sensors, your total material cost will be $5 million and your total labor cost will be $2 million. If you sell 1.5 million sensors, your total material cost will be $7.5 million and your total labor cost will be $3 million. Because the total cost varies with the number of units sold, these costs are considered variable.

Period Costs

Your business has other costs that do not vary with the level of sales. While variable costs are measured according to how much business is done (costs that vary by level of sales), period costs measure costs over a specific period of time.

For Example:

> A period cost in your non-business life would be your apartment rent. If you rent an apartment, the cost of rent does not go up or down depending on how many nights you spend in the apartment. The amount of rent is fixed for this period of time, in this case, one month. You must pay the full month's rent regardless of how many night you have stayed in your apartment.

Over the course of the first year, you spend $800,000 on research and development to improve your electronic sensor. You do this because you will have to change your product over time to remain attractive to your customers. This amount comes out of cash and also out of the owners' earnings. (This keeps the balance statement balanced!)

In a similar way, you spend $1.2 million on advertising and another $1 million on developing your relationships with your customers. This supports your sales budget and the way that you get product to your customers through the channels of distribution as you support the efforts of your sales force. These expenses are paid out of cash and also reduce the owners' earnings.

Assets				Liabilities			Owners' Equity	
Cash	Acct. Rec.	Inv.	Plant/Equip.	Acct. Pay	ST Debt	LT Debt	PIC	Earnings
$5,000		$12,000	$18,000	$2,000	$4,000	$9,000	$20,000	
15,000								15,000
	5,000							5,000
		(10,000)						(10,000)
(4,000)								(4,000)
(800)								(800)
(1,200)								(1,200)
(1,000)								(1,000)
$13,000	$5,000	$2,000	$18,000	$2,000	$4,000	$9,000	$20,000	$3,000

For convenience, as you continue accounting for business operations (revenues and expenses), only the account balances (above) will be carried over in the next worksheets.

Your goal is to accurately account for the value of the wealth that you are using and creating. A difficult problem is accounting for using up, or consuming, the value of your equipment. This is called ***depreciation***.

Consider the example of a truck:

> You purchase a new truck for $25,000. You expect it to last for five years and to have no value at the end of the five years, which is called its residual value. When you purchase the truck, your "Plant and Equipment" account shows this $25,000 value. The problem is that at the end of the first year, the truck is no longer worth $25,000, it is in fact worth less. Since it has a projected life of five years, you have consumed one-fifth (1/5 of $25,000 = $5,000) of the total value. To account for this consumption of value, you create a new asset account called Accumulated Depreciation.
>
> At the end of the first year, the truck's $25,000 value is reduced by $5,000. At the end of the second year, the reduction is $10,000; at the end of the third year, it is $15,000; at the end of the fourth year, it is $20,000; and at the end of the fifth year, it has become a$25,000 reduction.

There are a variety of ways to depreciate your capital equipment. The simplest is called ***straight-line depreciation***. You start with the purchase price ($18 million) and subtract how much it will be worth at the end of its useful life, or its residual value. The difference is "consumed" equally over each year of the plant's or equipment's useful life. You expect to be able to use your current plant and equipment for 10 years. At the end of the 10 years, it will have a residual value of $8 million.

$18M (purchase) - $8M (residual value) = $10M

$10M of value consumed over 10 years = $1M per year

The depreciation expense does not reduce the amount of cash on hand (it is a non-cash expense), but it does reduce the value of the assets you have control over. It also reduces the value of the owners' wealth in the company and, therefore, reduces earnings.

Assets					Liabilities			Owners' Equity	
Cash	Acct. Rec.	Inv.	Plant/ Equip.	Ac. Depr.	Acct. Pay	ST Debt	LT Debt	PIC	Earnings
$13,000	$5,000	$2,000	$18,000		$2,000	$4,000	$9,000	$20,000	$3,000
				(1,000)					(1,000)
$13,000	$5,000	$2,000	$18,000	($1,000)	$2,000	$4,000	$9,000	$20,000	$2,000

Paying Loan Principal and Interest

At the end of the year, you have to pay the "rent" for using other people's money (interest on the loan) and give back some of the money you are using. These amounts were specified in the original loan agreements or contracts. Over the past year, you incurred an interest expense on $13 million worth of loans. You agreed to pay the owners of that money 10% of the total value to be able to use it (10% of $13 million is $1.3 million). This comes out of cash and is an expense that reduces the value of the owners' earnings. This is just one of the costs of being in business.

At the end of the year, you have $4 million in loans that have to be paid back. According to the loan agreements (contracts) you signed, you do not have the right to use this money any longer. This $4 million comes out of cash and reduces the amount of debt that your company has. This return of money reduces the total value of the company; that is, it reduces the amount of wealth that you control and can use to do business. However, it is *not* an expense and therefore does *not reduce* the owners' wealth.

Assets					Liabilities			Owners' Equity	
Cash	Acct. Rec.	Inv.	Plant/Equ ip.	Ac. Depr.	Acct. Pay	ST Debt	LT Debt	PIC	Earnings
$13,000	$5,000	$2,000	$18,000	($1,000)	$2,000	$4,000	$9,000	$20,000	$2,000
(1,300)									(1,300)
(4,000)						(4,000)			
$7,700	$5,000	$2,000	$18,000	($1,000)	$2,000	0	$9,000	$20,000	$700

Financial Statement Conclusion

Each of the account balances changes when certain transactions take place. A ***Balance Sheet*** is a summary of the account balances at a specific point in time. It is a "snapshot" of the company's financial condition and summarizes all of the transactions that have occurred from the start of the company until that point in time. Two of the accounts, Cash and Retained Earnings, can provide additional useful information if they are summarized separately. Transactions over a specific period of time that affect the Retained Earnings account are summarized in an ***Income Statement***. This statement details the revenues coming into the company and the expenses occurred by the company during that time period. It is possible to make money (have positive earnings) and still run out of cash. If you run out of cash, you cannot continue to do business. The ***Statement of Cash Flow*** shows the changes in your cash account over a period of time.

Investment Financing: Getting Money to Grow Your Business

Companies that are growing always need more money to fuel their growth. They need money to develop new products, to buy new equipment, and to take advantage of opportunities in the market as they emerge.

Individuals or organizations who might provide money that will allow you to grow your business want something from you. It is an economic transaction that follows the rules of all economic transactions. People will only participate if they are made better off through the transaction.

There are basically two kinds of transactions that will get you the money:

Taking out a loan (debt contract), and;

Taking on new owners.

Both of these transactions provide cash to help the business thrive. In all other ways they are quite different.

For example:

If I have money to invest, it represents wealth that I have created in the past and not yet consumed. I could use that wealth to buy tools that would allow me to create something of value that I could take to the market. This investment in myself would give me a greater ability to create wealth in the future. However, if I am not going to use it myself, I still want to put it to work. I want that money to work for me as hard as it can, 24 hours a day. One of the things I can do is let others use my money to create wealth that will come back to me in some form.

If I am a person who has money to invest, what do I want out of the transaction? I want the highest return I can get for my money, and I want to be sure that I do not lose my money. The degree of certainty (or uncertainty) that I will get my money back is the "risk." In a market system, I have a lot of choices about how to put my money to work.

I might be attached to my money and only want it to work in a safe and secure environment. If that is what I want, I would only "rent" my money to people who were going to use it conservatively. Maybe I would rent it to the government, which can guarantee its safe return. The problem is that everything else being equal (which it isn't) there are a lot of people willing to put their money out for a safe use. When there is a lot of money competing to be put to a safe use, it is easy for those "safe users" (for example, electric utilities or governments) to get the use of that money cheaply. For the person investing the money, therefore, the "return" is expected to be low.

On the other hand, I might be willing to risk my money and give it to someone who will use it in a venture that just might not work out economically. It may represent a risk. For instance, I might put my money to work in a biotech firm. They always need more money to create useful mutant biological stuff. The problem is that at this point, a low percentage of biotech projects work out. However, the ones that do work out economically make huge amounts of money. To rent your money or attract your interest, they have to offer you a high return on your money.

The common rule is:

The higher the risk, the greater the expected return.

Loans

A loan is basically a form of a rental agreement. If I were borrowing money from you, I would be renting the use of your wealth (the amount borrowed is the principal of the loan). At the end of that loan period, I would be expected to return your wealth in good condition. I am renting your money for a specific period of time (term of the loan) and paying you a fee for the use (interest) of that money. Almost always, the fee for using other people's wealth is a percentage of the money you are renting and called the interest rate.

In business, your venture's risk can be a function of the industry you are in, your strategy for competing in that industry, and your experience in serving this market. Your financing strategy, or the way you go about getting the money you need to grow your business, also influences your risk. The more debt you have the more risk you are exposed to. Debt involves a contract whose terms you must meet. If you do not meet your obligation (make your payment), the contract usually specifies a remedy. This may include your creditor's being able to force you to sell your assets until you can meet your contractual obligations. When this happens, you are in the process of going out of business. The greater the percentage of assets acquired by debt, the greater the possibility that you would be forced to sell key assets to meet your obligations.

In Foundation™

All companies in Foundation face the same level and type of market risk. Therefore, the proportion of your assets that are financed by debt determines your risk level. Your company's risk is measured by the debt-to-assets ratio. When your debt-to-assets ratio approaches 80%, the banks will not lend you additional funds, and they will charge you the highest interest rate possible. Keeping your debt-to-assets ratio at an acceptable level—below 80% in this case—will allow you to have access to more affordable capital that you can use to operate and expand your business.

Borrowing money increases the total value of your company and infuses cash into the business, but this money is not income. The transaction involves increasing the balance of your cash account and increasing the value of the appropriate liability account. Paying back the loan reduces the balance in your cash account (and the value of your company) and the balance in the appropriate liability account.

IMPORTANT:

Paying down the principal of a loan is not an expense. However, the interest that you pay to use or "rent" the money is a legitimate business expense. Interest expenses reduce the balance in your cash account and the balance in your retained earnings account. Because is comes out of retained earnings, it is a part of (and expensed on) the income statement and reduces your net profits. The more you borrow, the higher the interest rate and the higher the interest payment.

In Foundation™

You can borrow money in four ways:

1. Purchase inventory *(materials)* on credit from your suppliers *(short term)*
2. Take a short-term loan *(1 year)* from the bank
3. Take a long-term loan from the market *(selling a long-term debt called a bond.)*
4. Take an emergency loan *(a short-term loan that is very expensive!)*

Instead of going out of business and instead of selling off your assets, you may be forced to take out an emergency loan. This is an expensive loan that you must pay back within the next year, and it drives your interest rates up. You want to avoid an emergency loan whenever possible by using solid financing strategies as you invest in your business.

Accounts Payable

When you purchase materials on account you increase the balance in your inventory account and you increase the balance in your accounts payable account. You are borrowing the use of materials from your suppliers to create products. When you sell the products, you will have the required cash to pay back your suppliers. As mentioned earlier, the amount of time you can use these materials for is called the Accounts Payable lag. As your A/P lag gets larger, your suppliers become more reluctant to provide more materials. If you do not have the materials, you cannot produce product, and the actual number of units produced in a period is decreased and reflected on the production strategy sheet.

Short-Term Bank Loans

Banks are financial institutions that accept deposits and make loans. They fall into several categories, such as savings and loans, thrift institutions, and commercial banks. Knowing the category in which they include themselves can tell you a lot about the kinds of loans these banks are interested in making. Savings banks are more experienced in dealing with consumer loans, such as home mortgages and automobile loans. Commercial banks have more experience and interest in business loans. The most important point to keep in mind when dealing with a bank is that bankers avoid risk. Their primary concern is always the safety of their funds. A bank will have a company fill out an application, document their financial history (past balance sheets and income statements), and submit a business plan to assess future potential financial success. In Foundation, your risk is determined by the percentage of assets that are financed by loans, determined by the debt-to-assets ratio.

A Short-Term Loan

In the real world, if you run out of money, you have to sell assets to meet your obligations. If you sell assets that you could use productively, you are in the business of going out of business.

Bonds

A bond is a form of long-term financing. When you borrow money from a bank, you sign a debt contract to use the bank's money for a certain period of time and to pay a specific rate of interest. You might have to pledge specific assets as security, or collateral, for the loan. If you should miss payments, the bank can force you to sell the asset and use that money to retire the loan. The terms of this contract are set for the duration of the loan.

Companies and government entities can develop a similar debt contract, but instead of borrowing money from a bank, they can borrow money directly from investors. These debt contracts are called bonds. Bonds are referred to as *securities* because they represent secured (or asset-based) claims for the investors. Stocks are another type of security---secured or asset-based claims against the company. Both are traded in *securities markets.*

The debt contract is called an "indenture" and contains the critical information of a loan including answers to these questions:

Who is borrowing the money?

How much money is being borrowed?

For what period of time?

At what rate of interest?

How and when is the loan going to be paid off?

How will the loan amount be secured?

When you borrow money from a bank, you provide information in the loan application that helps the bank determine how likely you are to meet the terms of the contract. The bank uses this assessment to determine whether or not to loan you the money and how high an interest rate they should charge. The higher the risk of nonpayment, the higher the interest rate you have to pay.

It is impractical for every investor who might want to buy a bond (loan some money) to assess the risk of the company (or government entity) who is issuing the bond. Instead, a few well-established companies, such as Moody's and Standard & Poor's, will assess the company and the bond issue and assign it a risk rating. The ratings range from AAA, which is excellent, to D, which indicates a high level of risk.

Bond ratings progress from excellent to very poor in this order:

Bond Ratings		
Excellent	**AAA**	*Low Risk*
	AA	
	A	
	BBB	
	BB	
	B	
	CCC	
	CC	
	C	
	DDD	
	DD	
Very Poor	**D**	*High Risk*

The lower the bond rating the higher the interest rate the issuing company expects to pay in order to attract investors. Companies get very concerned when their bond rating is degraded. It communicates a negative message to the financial community and to the market in general.

The Bond Market

When bonds are first issued, the company who wants to issue the bond has to get permission from the *Securities and Exchange Commission* (a federal agency). The company then typically goes through an ***investment bank***. An investment bank is a financial institution that specializes in issuing and reselling new securities such as stocks and bonds. The financial managers of the company and the investment bankers go through the reasons for the bond issue (what are they borrowing money for), how long they want to borrow the money for, how much money they want, and how much interest they expect to pay.

The investment bank then works to market the new bond issue. They contact big investors—such as banks, insurance companies, pension funds—to determine the willingness of the market to buy the bonds and to create a distribution network for the bond issue. They also *underwrite* (buy) a significant portion of the bond issue. This first sale of the newly issued security takes place in the ***primary securities market***.

Because bonds are a secured claim, investors who own them can buy and sell them to other investors. These transactions occur in the ***secondary securities markets (or exchanges)*** or the "bond market." In the bond market, the bond (debt contract) can trade above or below the face value of the bond. In general, bond prices move in the opposite direction of interest rates—as interest rates fall, bond prices go up, and as interest rates rise, bond prices drop.

A bond is an investment whose return is specified in the debt contract. Consider a very simple example: A $1,000 bond that pays 10% interest per year for 5 years.

As an investor, you see the investment like this:

YEARS	"Bond A"
Year 1	$100
Year 2	$100
Year 3	$100
Year 4	$100
Year 5	$100 + $1,000
TOTAL	**$1,500**

Because this is a contract, this return on your investment does not vary at all. Suppose as an investor, you had the opportunity to choose between buying the 5-year, 10% bond or a new, 5-year, 15% bond (assume equal "risk" or bond rating). If the two investments looked like this, which would you choose?

YEARS	"Bond A"	"Bond B"
Year 1	$100	$150
Year 2	$100	$150
Year 3	$100	$150
Year 4	$100	$150
Year 5	$100 + $1,000	$150 + $1,000
TOTAL	**$1,500**	**$1,750**

The rational investor would pick the investment with the higher return: "Bond B" paying 15% interest. However, if the investor who owned "Bond "A" was motivated, she might offer to sell it at $980. If she attracted no buyers, she might offer it at $960, then $940, and then at some lower price. The potential buyer would then be as well off buying "Bond A" as "Bond B." As the return on the alternative investment (interest rate of the other bond) goes up, the trading price of existing bonds goes down.

Consider the same scenario, but the alternative bond offers a 5-year, 5% return:

YEARS	"Bond A"		"Bond C"
Year 1	$100		$50
Year 2	$100		$50
Year 3	$100		$50
Year 4	$100		$50
Year 5	$100 + $1,000		$50 + $1,000
TOTAL	**$1,500**		**$1,250**

The rational investor would want to buy bond "A," as would other investors. The current owner of "Bond A" faces a situation where there are motivated buyers competing to buy his investment. The owner would then bid the price of a 10% bond higher than the face value ($1,000) because the return is better than any alternatives. At some price, say $1,120 for discussion purposes, the two investments would be equally attractive and would generate buyers. A $1,120 price for a bond that pays $1,500 would be about as attractive as a $1,000 price for a bond that pays $1,250.

Bonds are bought and sold every day on the bond market. At the end of a trading day, the information about the outstanding bonds, the value of their issue, their trading prices, yield, and the bond rating of the company are published in the financial press, as per the following example:

Company	Issue	Value	Yield	Close	S&P
Digby	10.8S2013	$4,347,878	10.3%	105.16	AA
	13.2S2014	$23,000,000	11.4%	115.48	AA

In this instance, the company "Digby" has two different issues of bonds outstanding.

The first bond "10.8S2013" is:

An issue that pays 10.8% each year until the bond matures in 2013.
One that when the series was issued, Digby received $4,347,878.
Currently trading at 105.16% of its face value.
Showing a face value of $1,000, so it would currently cost you $1,051.60 to purchase one of these bonds.
One with a 10.8% return on a price of $1,051.60, so it's real return, or yield, 10.3%.

The second bond "13.2S2014" is:

An issue that pays 13.2% each year until the bond matures in 2014.
A significant issue, raising $23 million.
Currently trading at $1,154.80 for a $1,000 face-value bond.
Showing a purchase price of $1,154.80 on a 13.2% bond and providing a real yield of 11.4%.

The company has an AA bond rating based on its current financial status.

In Foundation™

When you sell new bond issues, the interest rate you have to pay is 1.4% higher than your short-term rate. You would choose to do this if you thought you might have to borrow more money in the future. The more you borrow, the higher your risk and the higher the interest payment you have to pay. It does not take very long before your short-term rate will be above the 1.4% premium, making the earlier decision to "lock in" an interest rate for the term of the bond a better decision. When you issue new bonds, there is a commission that you have to pay to the investment bankers to help you issue the new bonds. The year your bonds mature, they are transferred from long-term debt to short-term debt and automatically paid off. The amount you pay is the value of the bond issue as shown in column 3. Your bond price goes up and down depending on the interest rate. If you want to retire bonds, or buy back your bonds before they come to maturity, you have to pay the closing price.

Stockowner's Equity

When you sell shares of stock, you are selling ownership rights to a corporation. Owners, or stockholders, never have to be paid back, and you do not have to pay them interest on the money that they are investing in the company. However, owners have a claim against the assets and the wealth that is created in the form of net income, earnings, and profit by the company. That ownership claim *never* ends. This ownership lasts as long as the organization does, and the owners will continue to have a say in the management of the company.

Stock Market

When you own a stock, you are actually a part-owner of a corporation. As a shareholder, you have a "say" in how the company operates, although your voice may be just one among thousands of other shareholders.

Companies initially issue stock to raise capital to run their businesses, often motivated by the fact that they need more money. A corporation sells shares to investors in an organized fashion called a public offering, the first of which is its initial public offering, or ***IPO***. After the company's IPO, investors are free to sell their shares and buy more, but not from the company directly. Instead, shares are traded on organized stock markets like the New York Stock Exchange and NASDAQ.

A company can issue common stock or preferred stock. ***Common stock*** represents a simple share of ownership and each common stock share has one vote to cast when electing the corporation's board of directors. If the company were to go bankrupt, the corporation would have no financial liability to common shareholders, and those shares may become worthless. ***Preferred stock***, a form of stock that is traded at a far lower volume than common stock, does have privileges. Preferred shareholders, often having some kind of history or relationship within the company, may receive higher dividends and have a first claim to assets if a company should go bankrupt.

Shares of stock are traditionally represented by a piece of paper called a stock certificate. Since shares of stock trade electronically, you may never actually see a physical certificate for the share that you own. The brokerage holds the shares on your behalf in what is known as a "street name," which is nothing more than a method of bookkeeping and has no effect on your ownership of the stock. Owning shares in street name is much more efficient and convenient, especially when it is time to sell the stock.

Like a bond, stocks are secured investments. They have a claim against the assets of the company. The company sells new shares of stock to potential owners through the ***primary securities market*** in a process similar to the way new bond issues are sold. The company meets with an investment banker who reviews the business strategy and specific plans for the money that is to be raised. The investment bank underwrites or buys, markets and distributes the new shares. Underwriters charge a commission and also make money by holding some of the shares until the price per share rises. Again, once stock has been issued, owners can buy from and sell to others on the ***secondary securities markets*** *(exchanges)* in "stock markets" in the United States and in numerous exchanges throughout the world. The company itself receives no cash for shares that are sold in the secondary markets, and every corporation wants to see its stock price increase for the benefit of its shareholders and the financial reputation of the corporation.

If you are a potential investor in a company (someone who is thinking about purchasing shares of stock in a company), you have choices about which company you might want to purchase shares in. You want to invest your money in a company that is going to work your money and create as much wealth for you as possible.

There are two ways in which your wealth increases by owning stock:

When the value of your shares increases as the stock price goes up

When the company distributes the profits it has created in the form of cash payments called dividends to owners out of net income.

Paying Dividends

When a company creates profit, the profit belongs to the owners. There are only two things that can happen with that profit:

It can be kept in the company as retained earnings

It can be distributed to the owners in the form of a cash disbursement or payment. If it is paid out to the owners, it reduces the amount of cash on hand.

For example:

As an owner, I might wish to invest in a company that pays a regular dividend. For instance, if I were retired I might want to have 10,000 shares of stock in a company that regularly pays a four dollar per share dividend. I would know that every year, I would receive $40,000 in cash for me to live on. I would think about this dividend policy added to the value of the shares of stock I purchased and would consider this in deciding how much I might be willing to pay for that stock.

In Foundation™

Dividends should be paid from the profits of the business. It is generally not a good idea to pay dividends in a year when you are borrowing money. Owners and the market for potential owners interpret this as borrowing money to pay the dividend. The owners gave the managers of the company their money to grow their wealth, not for the managers to take out loans in their name. Owners do not like managers to hold "excessive" cash balances. It is the owners' money, and they expect it to be working hard to create more wealth. Cash does not earn any return. Owners think that if you do not have a productive use for their cash, you should give it back to them by paying a dividend. A "productive use" is to invest it in new products, make facility improvements, or act on other decisions that will put that cash to work for the business.

Ratios, Value, and Stock Claims

The interaction of buyers and sellers of the stock determine stock price. A potential buyer might consider three things in determining how much they would be willing to pay to own stock in a particular company:

The value of the stock's claim against the assets of the company

How much profit the company makes per share of stock

How much of that profit is distributed to owners (in form of a dividend)

The value of this claim is determined by dividing the total owners' equity from the balance sheet by the number of shares outstanding. For instance, if the value of the owners' claim is $100 million and there are 2 million shares of stock issued and outstanding, then each share has a claim against the assets of the company worth $50. This is called the ***book value*** of the stock.

There are two ways to increase book value:

Increase the value of total owners' equity
Reduce the number of shares outstanding (buy back stock)

The easiest way to increase owners' equity is to make a profit and reinvest it, or retain it, in the company, which increases the value of the "retained earnings" account. If you sell more shares to increase the value of the common stock account, you have increased the value of total owners' equity, but you have also increased the number of shares you have to divide it by in order to get book value. In general, current owners would prefer that you borrow money to grow the company, if you can afford the interest payments, rather than dilute the value of their claim.

Leverage

The concept of **leverage** measures how big of a company the managers have created using the owners' investments. Leverage is measured with the following equation:

Leverage = Total Assets / Total Owner's Equity

Assume that owners have invested a total of $1 million. In this first example, the managers have created a company whose total assets are $1.5 million. The leverage ratio is 1.5.

$1.5 million / $1 million = 1.5

How could the managers create a $1.5 million company with owners' investments of $1 million? Remember, the accounting equation is:

Assets = Liabilities + Owners' Equity

One way they can accomplish this is by borrowing the $.5 million. The managers have created a company 1.5 times as big as the owners' investments by borrowing additional capital.

In the second example, the managers have created a company whose total assets are $5 million from the initial $1 million invested. Therefore, the leverage ratio is 5.

$5 million / $1 million = 5

Managers in this company used the initial $1 million investment to borrow an additional $4 million. They created a company five times as big as the owners' investments.

In general, as an owner with a $1 million investment, one would rather own a $5 million company than a $1.5 million company. It is desirable to borrow money rather than to sell stock, as long as it makes economic sense.

Measuring Profit per Share

The goal of a business is to make a profit. Interest payments on loans reduce profits. As an owner, I am interested in how much new wealth (profit) the company makes per share of stock. I want them to make as much as possible. Earnings per share (EPS) is a ratio that calculates profit per share:

EPS = Net Income / Number of shares

If a company with 1 million shares of stock outstanding creates a net income of $10 million, the EPS would be $10 per share. Clearly, the way to maximize this number is to make as much profit as possible while keeping the number of shares as low as possible. In addition, remember that owners have a claim against all future profits of the company. The company made $10 per share this year, an owner might anticipate earnings at least that good in the future. This anticipation of future earnings also influences how the value of a share is determined.

Stock Reports

Large volumes of stock are commonly traded every day. At the end of the day, the transactions in the market are summarized so investors can study what has been happening and make informed decisions about future purchases.

Company	Close	Change	Shares	Dividend	Yield	P/E	EPS
Andrews	$51.29	$22.48	2,000,000	$2.00	3.9%	5.8	$8.88
Baldwin	$69.86	$21.09	2,157,790	$0.50	0.7%	5.6	$12.49
Chester	$41.26	$6.75	2,045,860	$1.00	2.4%	6.8	$6.04
Digby	$37.40	$10.60	4,096,380	$2.00	5.3%	8.1	$4.61
Erie	$15.82	($0.47)	3,209,871	$0.00	0.0%	18.0	$0.88
Ferris	$65.20	$24.76	2,339,022	$3.00	4.6%	6.0	$10.84

In the above table, the trading of six companies' stocks is summarized. Let's use the first one, Andrews, as an example:

- At the end of the trading day, Andrews' stock was selling at (that is, valued by buyers at) $51.29 per share.
- Because this is $22.48 higher than the close at the end of the last trading period, the last closing price was $28.81 ($28.81 + $22.48 = $51.29).
- Andrews has 2 million shares of stock outstanding. Last year, they paid a dividend of $2.00 to each of those 2 million shareholders (which would reduce their cash by $4 million ($2 x 2 million).
- This $2.00 payment represents a 3.9% return (yield) on the $51.29 stock price: (2 / 51.29 = .03899 or approximately 3.9%).

Therefore, each share of Andrews' outstanding stock (2 million) has earned $8.88 of net income (Earnings per Share). Their total net income must have been $17.76 million (2 million x $8.88).

The ratio in the next to the last column is the ***Price/Earnings*** ratio, or the ***PE***, which measures how many times you would have to multiply the earnings to get the stock price. Andrews' stock is trading at 5.8 times as much as it earned in this one year.

Other Important Ratios

Investments in current assets represent a substantial portion of a small business's total assets: up to 70 percent of total business spending may be used for purchases of supplies and raw materials. Additionally, about 40 percent of a typical firm's capital is represented by its current assets value. Therefore, proper management and use of current assets and current liabilities is crucial to the health and survival of any small business.

Three ratios allow a comparison of your business with your competitors' and to industry averages. These ratios also play an important role in the granting or denial of loan requests. Managers should calculate and monitor these financial ratios as part of their working-capital management policy.

Current Ratio

Current Assets / Current Liabilities

Quick (or Acid) Ratio

(Current Assets - Inventories) / Current Liabilities

Total-Debt-to-Total-Assets Ratio

Total Debt / Total Assets

The Current and Quick ratios measure liquidity and reveal whether the firm can meet its debts for the coming year. The Debt-to-Asset Ratio shows the degree of financial leverage.

Using the Cash-Flow Statement as a Management Tool

It is important that managers ensure that the business always has enough cash on hand to purchase and pay for the materials and human resources it needs to produce goods and services. The cash-flow statement can be a valuable tool to determine how much cash is available now and how much will be available in the future and when. This activity, called cash-flow management, requires careful planning. Although sales may be booming, if sufficient cash is not available to pay the expenses for the month, the firm will not have funds to pay for them. This may result in a costly "emergency loan" or potentially a bankruptcy. If excess cash balances are allowed to sit idle instead of being invested, a firm loses the potential opportunity for cash returns that it might have otherwise earned.

Review and Discussion Questions

1. What is a dividend?

2. What does earnings per share measure?

3. How is capital acquired through the finance department?

4. If you sell products on credit, how is that transaction recorded?

5. What does return on sales (ROS) measure and what relevance might that provide?

6. What insight might return on equity (ROE) provide?

7. What does leverage measure? What might a radical change in leverage from year to year indicate?

8. Discuss the potential relationship between gross sales and profits.

9. What does stock represent?

10. What might be the ramifications, financially and from a marketing perspective, of increasing the account receivable lag time?

Chapter **7**

Business and Society: The Legal and Regulatory System

The private enterprise system requires laws to make corrections when markets do not produce the outcomes desirable for the people in a society.

Key terms to look for:

- Administrative law
- Agency
- Arbitration
- Civil law
- Common law
- Contract law
- Criminal law
- Expressed warranty
- Fraud
- Limited warranty
- Mediation
- Statutory law
- Tort

Our society has agreed to live by a set of rules or laws that ensure that the conditions necessary for free private enterprise exist and are protected. These rules or laws are set by the customs of the society or through the action of the government, which acts as the agent for the society. While the law establishes the private enterprise system, it also corrects for the times when markets fail or when markets do not produce the outcomes most desired by the people in a society.

Chapter 1 discussed the four conditions required for the private enterprise system to work:

- Right to private property
- Right to keep profits
- Freedom of Choice
- Fair competition

These four conditions, necessary for the private enterprise system to function, are established in different bodies of law. When these conditions exist, competition for transactions in markets will create pressure for innovation and low prices and result in an efficient allocation of goods. As a society, we value these outcomes.

Freedom of choice is established in the Constitution of the United States as an underlying principle upon which the country was founded. It is not within the scope of this course to review the body of laws guaranteeing choice.

The right to *private property* and the right to *keep profits* are defined in a body of property law. ***Property law*** establishes the rights of a person to own, use, transfer, and captures the economic value of different kinds of property. It recognizes that property can be *tangible* (that is, has a physical existence, such as a car) and *intangible* (such as a trademark or stock in a corporation). Property law establishes:

- ***Real property***: real estate and everything attached to it
- ***Personal property***: property other than real property
- ***Intellectual property***: property generated by a person's creative activities. Copyrights protect the ownership of property such as books, music, and software. Patents give an inventor the exclusive right to exploit an invention for a period of time. A trademark provides legal protection to a created identity or brand. This may be based upon a name, a mark, or a symbol.

Fair competition is established in a wide variety of law and regulation. In general, fair competition is broadly established in laws that prevent businesses from:

- Restraining trade and monopolizing markets (Sherman Antitrust Act), and
- Price discrimination, tying, exclusive agreements that substantially lessen competition (Clayton Act).

All areas of law that influence business practice contribute to our shared definition of fairness. Examples are the laws and regulations that establish standards of conducts in negotiating contracts with a company's buyers or suppliers, providing information (advertising) to consumers, providing information to potential investors, and negotiating with employees or their representatives.

Contract Law

The heart of the private enterprise system is the transaction, or the mutual agreement of exchange. Virtually every transaction is carried out by means of a contract. A contract is a mutual agreement between two or more parties whose terms are enforceable in court. A contract does not have to be written. It is any agreement that meets three criteria, which are called elements and include:

- ***Voluntary agreement***: The offer and acceptance have to be freely and knowingly made; it is not a contract if any party uses fraud or force to come to agreement.
- ***Consideration***: To be a contract, the agreement to exchange must involve something of economic value (money, goods, or services). Therefore, the word *consideration* is another term for *money.*
- ***Contractual capacity***: To be a contract, both parties must have a legal ability to enter into the contract. Individuals who are minors (under the age of 18), mentally unstable, retarded, insane, or intoxicated lack the capacity to enter into a legal contract.

The failure to live up to the terms agreed upon in a contract is called breach of contract. If arbitration is not used, a court can order the terms of the contract to be met and damages to be paid if the breach resulted in monetary damages.

Sources of Law

How did the "rules" of our society come into existence? There are three sources:

Statutory law: written laws established by federal, state, county, or city governments

Common law: unwritten laws that are established by judicial decisions; such law in the United States was inherited from English law

Administrative law: regulations established by administrative agencies

Dispute Resolution

Whenever there are individuals acting in their own best interest, there will be conflict. As standards of behavior are established, there will be disputes over whether specific behaviors meet those standards. There are two kinds of disputes:

Disputes between and individual and the government

Disputes between two individuals. ("Individuals" can be any form of private party and can include different kinds of businesses).

A dispute between the government and an individual over whether behavior meets the set standards is a matter of ***criminal law***. Violation of criminal law is called a crime and may be punished by fines and/or imprisonment. A dispute between two individuals is considered a matter of ***civil law***. Violations of civil law may result in fines but not imprisonment.

Violations of criminal law are resolved through the court system. Each level of government (federal, state, and city levels, for example) has its own courts to resolve violations of the laws that they establish. ***Trial courts*** determine the facts of a case, the laws that pertain, and apply the law to resolve the dispute. If either party feels that the law was misinterpreted or misapplied, they can appeal the decision to an ***appellate court***. Court judgments are binding and are enforced through the power of the government.

When two individuals have a dispute, it is called a civil dispute. Civil disputes are initiated and resolved through ***lawsuits***. Lawsuits are the main remedy for business disputes. As with criminal law, they are resolved in trial and appellate courts.

Legal Options

The United States is a litigious society. This is a sophisticated way of saying we sue each other often. As a result of this demand and the consequent long delays in our court systems, alternative methods of dispute resolution are gaining popularity. These methods are typically faster and more cost effective than litigation through the traditional court system and include the following:

> ***Arbitration*** is a form of dispute resolution where the parties submit their case to a neutral third party called an arbitrator. The arbitrator decides how the dispute will be resolved and acts somewhat like a judge in the process. In most cases, arbitration is binding and requires the parties to accept the legally binding and enforceable solution. Either party may appeal the arbitrator's decision to a court but the court will generally not change the arbitrator's findings but decide only whether the arbitrator acted properly.
>
> ***Mediation*** is a form of negotiated resolution using a third party mediator to help reach an agreement. A neutral negotiator helps the two parties negotiate a settlement. Typically the mediator meets with each side separately until both sides agree to a settlement. Unlike arbitration, mediation is nonbinding, and neither side has the power of the courts to enforce the settlement. The dissatisfied party can take this case to court. In other words, the mediator functions more like a counselor than a judge, and the parties do not have to accept the mediator's decision.

Agency

Agency law allows an individual to assign to another person the power to act and to enter into agreements. The two parties (the principal and the agent) enter into an ***agency agreement***. The ***principal*** is the person who wishes to have a specific task accomplished, and the **agent** is the one who acts on the principal's behalf. ***Power of attorney*** is a legal document that authorizes a person to act as another's agent. A ***Partnership Agreement*** establishes a business partnership (form of organization) and creates mutual agency for the partners on behalf of the company.

Bankruptcy

If an individual or business cannot meet its contractual obligations based on available assets, it can declare bankruptcy as an option of last resort. Bankruptcy, or legal insolvency, asks a court to declare an individual or company unable to meet its contractual obligations and to release them from those obligations. The assets of the person or company declared bankrupt are sold to meet as much of the contractual obligation as possible. There are different kinds of bankruptcy:

- **Chapter 7** Requires that the business be dissolved and assets liquidated
- **Chapter 11** Temporarily frees the business from its obligations while it reorganizes and works out a court-approved plan for meeting its obligations
- **Chapter 13** Similar to Chapter 11, except it is limited to individuals versus businesses

Uniform Commercial Code

The laws governing business practice can come from many sources. States (except Louisiana) have adopted a consistent set of statutory laws that simplify commerce called the Uniform Commercial Code (UCC). As an example, the UCC has a section covering sales agreements, which are of course contracts. The UCC addresses the rights of buyers and sellers, transfers of ownership, the legal assumption of risk, and warranties. A warranty defines the terms that the seller will honor. All sales are covered by an ***implied warranty*** that allows the buyer to assume that:

The seller has clear title to the product (that is, it has not been stolen)

The product will perform the function for which it was produced and sold

It will perform as advertised

An "***expressed warranty***" covers any additional terms the seller will honor. An automobile manufacturer, for example, might offer a 5-year, 50,000-mile warranty on a vehicle during which it will fix any defects in the car.

TORTS AND FRAUD

As a society, we expect that the conduct of business will not "wrong" or harm others. A ***tort*** is a civil wrong (and includes all "wrongs" that are not breach of contract) in which one party through action or inaction causes harm to another. If a UPS driver, for example, loses control of a truck and causes injury to a person (or their property), that person can sue the driver and the company for damages.

Fraud is a criminal act, a form of a tort, in which one party in a transaction hurts another by purposefully deceiving or manipulating them. If a "travel agency" sold you a vacation package but never intended to deliver the plane tickets, that is fraud. If a hospital bills your insurance company for services that it did not provide, that is fraud. A criminal act and fraud convictions can result in imprisonment and fines.

An important part of tort law is ***product liability***, which establishes a business's legal responsibility to be diligent (not negligent) in the design, production, sale, and consumption of products. Liability often relies on the concept of what a *reasonable person* might expect to happen when using a product. For example, a reasonable person would expect a kitchen knife to be sharp and could not sue if he or she were cut while using it. A reasonable person would not expect a kitchen knife to break or separate from its handle in normal use and could sue if this happened and an injury or damage resulted.

FEDERAL ADMINISTRATIVE AGENCIES

Governments can pass a law that sets up an administrative agency that establishes operating rules (regulations) to guide business practices. Many agencies also have the power to resolve disputes involving their regulations. In these disputes, an administrative law judge decides the issues at a "hearing" rather than at a trial. Most agencies are established to regulate the practices within a specific industry, but some have authority in multiple industries and are called "cross-industry."

Cross-industry Agencies:

- Federal Trade Commission (FTC): business practices; false and deceptive advertising, labeling, and pricing
- Consumer Product Safety Commission (CPSC): consumer safety
- Occupational Safety and Health Administration (OSHA): worker safety issues
- Equal Employment Opportunity Commission (EEOC): employment discrimination
- Environmental Protection Agency (EPA): pollution standards

Industry Specific Agencies

- Food and Drug Administration (FDA): foods, drugs, and medical devices
- Interstate Commerce Commission (ICC): railroads, trucks, buses, ships
- Federal Communications Commission (FCC) wire, radio, TV, satellite, and cable
- Federal Energy Regulatory Commission (FERC): electricity, gas
- Federal Aviation Administration (FAA): airline industry
- Federal Highway Administration (FHA): vehicle and transportation safety
- Securities and Exchange Commission (SEC): corporate securities trading

Review and Discussion Questions

1. What are the requirements of a business contract and why are these important?

2. What are the differences between a criminal and civil law?

3. Describe the concept of agency and how it may be applied.

4. What is the primary reason for the existence of government and other regulatory organizations in business?

5. What are the two types of warranties and how do they vary?

6. What are the dispute resolution options and how might they impact legal options?

7. For what reasons might a person's contractual capacity be limited or nonexistent?

Chapter **8**

Forms of Business Organization

Business owners choose the most attractive form of the business ownership based on the number of owners, anticipated risk, expected profitability, and the potential future value of the firm.

Key terms to look for:

- Bylaws
- Common stock
- Corporation, or C Corporation
- Limited Liability Company
- Mutual agency
- Partnership
- Preferred stock
- S Corporation
- Sole proprietorship

When a business is established, the owners must decide on the form of ownership, a choice that affects both the owner and the business itself. This decision can be changed from one ownership form to another, but this may be complicated and potentially expensive with possible tax implications for owners. Therefore, this initial decision is an important one.[18]

There is no single "right" form of business organization, and the form of ownership that is best for one owner may not be suitable for another. Selecting the best form of ownership means that entrepreneurs must understand the characteristics of each form and how well those match the needs of their businesses. The most common considerations when evaluating the various forms of business ownership include:

> ***Tax considerations*** : The amount of net income an entrepreneur expects the business to generate and the tax bill the owner must pay are important factors.
>
> ***Liability exposure***: Certain forms of ownership offer business owners greater protection from personal liability that might result from financial problems, faulty products, and other potential difficulties.
>
> ***Start-up and future capital requirements:*** Forms of ownership differ in their ability to raise start-up and working capital.
>
> ***Control:*** An owner automatically gives up some control over the company by choosing certain forms of ownership.
>
> ***Managerial ability:*** The business owner may want to bring in other owners to provide a broader breadth of the necessary skills to successfully manage the venture.
>
> ***Business goals:*** The projected size of the business is another factor, and businesses often may switch forms of ownership as they grow, although moving from some formats to others can be extremely complex and expensive.
>
> ***Management succession plans***: When choosing a form of ownership, business owners must look ahead to the day when they will pass their companies on to the next generation or to a buyer.
>
> ***Cost of formation***: Owners must weigh carefully the benefits versus the costs of the particular form they choose.[19]

The organizational forms most commonly used by businesses in the United States fall into these general categories:

> Sole Proprietorship
>
> Partnership
>
> Corporation, also known as a C Corporation
>
> S Corporation
>
> Limited Liability Company

[18] Scarborough, Norman M., Doug Wilson, Thomas W. Zimmerer, *Essentials of Entrepreneurship and Small Business Management*, 5th edition. (Upper Saddle River, NJ: Pearson Education, 2008), page 160.
[19] Ibid.

To understand the differences between these forms and their advantages and disadvantages, you should know the answers to these questions:

- How are the profits and losses of the business taxed? *(taxes)*
- How is each type of legal organization set up? *(starting an organization)*
- Who owns the business? *(control)*
- Who is responsible if the business fails or has losses? *(liability)*
- How long does each type of organization last, and how does the owner sell the business? *(life of and sale of company)*

SOLE PROPRIETORSHIP

The sole proprietorship is the simplest and most common form of business organization. As its name implies, this business entity can have only one owner. This entity represents more than 70 percent of all businesses in the United States.[20] The primary advantages of the sole proprietorship are its:

Ease of formation
Least costly form of ownership to begin
Total decision-making authority and control
Minimal legal restrictions
Ease to discontinuing

The most significant disadvantages of a sole proprietorship are its:

Single owner status
Unlimited liability
The owner is individually responsible for all losses of the business
Limited skills and capabilities
Limited access to capital
Challenges in transitioning the business to other owners

Starting a Sole Proprietorship

You can start a sole proprietorship simply by registering your business name with the state you will operate in. A sole proprietorship is usually operated under the name of the individual owner, although you can choose another name. You should set up a system to keep track of your business's finances and keep records of all revenues and expenses. You should check with local government offices for information about licenses and permits. Examples of such include business licenses, zoning occupancy permits, and tax registrations.

Management and Control

If you create a sole proprietorship, all the assets of the business are owned directly by you. A sole proprietorship may be owned by only one person. The owner controls the business. You may hire employees to help manage your business, but you will have legal responsibility for the decisions made by your employees.

---

[20] Ibid, p. 163.

Liability

In a sole proprietorship, the owner and the business are legally the same. As the owner, you will have unlimited personal responsibility for your business's liabilities. For example, if your business cannot pay its loans, the bank can take action against you individually, against both the business's assets and your personal assets, including your bank account, car, and house.

The Life and Sale of a Sole Proprietorship

A sole proprietorship exists as long as its owner is alive and wants to continue the business. When the owner dies, the assets and liabilities of the business become part of the owner's estate. A sole proprietor is free to sell all or any part of the assets of the business.

Taxes

Because there is no legal difference between the person and the business, the business's income (minus allowable expenses) are reported on the owner's individual tax return and taxed at individual tax rates. No separate federal income tax return is required of the sole proprietor.

Sole Proprietorship Advantages	Sole Proprietorship Disadvantages
Inexpensive to start	Unlimited personal liability
Simple to run and administer	Ownership is limited to one person
Ease of formation	Most limited access to capital
Single (simple) taxation on profits	Challenging transition to a new owner

When multiple owners are desirable, a partnership is one way to overcome the disadvantages of sole proprietorship.

Terra Cycle *A business profile*

A high school plant project and a subsequent business plan competition led Tom Szaky and some friends to create a totally organic fertilizer. The group continued their pursuit of the stalled plant project as they left for college—Tom to Princeton University and his friends to McGill University in Montreal. It was then that one of the friends learned about fertilizing the plants with worm waste. He created a compost heap in a box, placed red worms in it, and started feeding them table scraps. Tom discovered that his friend Jon Beyer's father was an ecotoxicologist—a person who studies the effects of pollution on ecosystems. They thought the worm waste product was an excellent solution and subsequently, a business venture and a partnership of complementary skills was born.[21] Learn more about TerraCycle at www.terracycle.net.

PARTNERSHIPS

In the most general form, a partnership is created when two or more individuals agree to create a business and jointly own the assets, be responsible for the liabilities, and share both the profits and the losses. There are many different ways to structure a partnership, and you can limit a partner's "participation" (and their liability) in the partnership agreement.

[21] Bo Burlingham, "The Coolest Little Start-Up in America," *Inc. Magazine*, July 2006, page 78-83.

The advantages of a partnership are:

- Acquisition of complementary skills and talents
- Flexibility of division of profits
- Larger pool of capital with the ability to attract more partners
- Minimal government regulation

The disadvantage is that the general partners have:

- Unlimited liability of at least one partner who is personally responsible for the losses and other obligations
- Challenges in accumulating additional capital
- Difficulty in changing partners
- Potential lack of continuity
- Potential for personality and authority conflicts
- Bound by the law of agency

Starting a Partnership

You can start a general partnership by agreeing with one or more individuals to jointly own and share the profits of a business. You can form a partnership with other individuals, other partnerships, or with corporations. You can have as many partners as you want.

A partnership agreement, also known as the articles of partnership, outlines the exact status and responsibility of each partner. This document states the terms under which the partners agree to operate the business and protects each partner's interest in the business. Every partnership should be based on a written agreement that acts as a guide for the partners when they face challenging business decisions, such as how to distribute profits or how to sell or liquidate the business.[22]

The standard partnership agreement will likely include the following:

- Name of the partnership
- Purpose of the business
- Domicile of the business
- Duration of the partnership
- Names of the partners and their legal addresses
- Contributions of each partner to the business, at the creation of the partnership and later
- Agreement on how the profits or losses will be distributed
- Agreement on salaries or drawing rights against profits for each partner
- Procedure of expansion through the addition of new partners
- Sale of partnership interests
- Salaries, draws, and expense accounts for the partners
- Absence or disability of one of the partners
- Dissolution of the partnership and distribution of assets

[22] Ibid, p. 166.

The partnership agreement should specify who controls and manages the business. If there is a need to limit the participation and liability of a partner, those limits should be established in the partnership agreement. The law assumes "general" participation unless specific statutory requirements are met, so it is important to have a lawyer review the agreement. In the absence of a specific agreement, all general partners have equal control and equal management rights over the business. This means that all of the partners must consent and agree to partnership decisions. If the purpose of limiting the partnership is to limit the liability of a partner, then the limited partner must have limited managerial control as well. The premise of a partnership is that partners are responsible, and protection from responsibility cannot be given to active decision makers. This and other partner provisions must be specified in the partnership agreement.

A partnership may operate under the names of the partners. Some states require partnerships to file partnership certificates, often with the secretary of state's office. If the partners' names are not used, a "doing business as" form may need to be filed. The partnership should set up a system to keep track of the business's finances and keep records of all revenues and expenses so the partners know whether there are profits and how they accrue to the individual partner.

Frontera Foods *A business profile*

The partners at Frontera Foods are in a perpetual creative struggle—with each other. "We are very different," concedes Rick Bayless as he thinks of his partner Manuel Valdes. Bayless's talents come out in the kitchen, Valdes has the business sense. The trio of successful companies the two co-founded and run—Frontera Foods, Frontera Media Productions, and Frontera Fresco–now exceed $15 million in annual sales. Over the past decade, the partners have butted heads and the creative tug-of-wars continue. "I'm ready to kill an idea," says Valdes, "and he's ready to do it another way." Based on the performance of their businesses, they would not have it any other way.[23] Learn more about Frontera Foods at www.fronterafoods.com.

Management and Control

The partnership agreement defines the percentage of the business and profits each partner will own. The law may assume that each partner will have an equal claim on the assets of the business, its profits, and its liabilities. Most partnership agreements are negotiated on the principle of a proportional claim based on the cumulative investments of the partner.

Mutual agency

Partnerships are based on the concept of mutual agency. The partnership is held responsible for the decisions and behavior of each partner (this is an example of "a chain is only as strong as its weakest link" principle). Any partner can bind the partnership to contracts or legal obligations without the approval of the other partners. Any partner can expose the partnership to criminal or civil actions.

[23] Emily Lambert, "The Odd Couple," *Forbes*, September 4, 2006, p. 73

Unlimited Liability of General Partners

A general partnership has some characteristics of a legal entity that is separate from its owners. For instance a partnership can own property and conduct business. However, the general partners have unlimited personal liability and are in an agency relationship with all other partners. All of the partners are liable together and each general partner is individually liable for any and all of the obligations of the partnership. This means, for example, that partner A could borrow money in the name of the partnership and the creditor could require other partners individually to pay back the money. If partner B cannot pay back the money partner A has borrowed, partner B's personal assets (home, car, etc.) might be used to meet this obligation.

Limited Liability of Limited Partners

Limited partners do not have personal liability for the business of the partnership. Limited partners risk only their investment in (or specified contributions to) the partnership.

The Life and Sale of a Partnership

A partnership lasts as long as the partners agree it will or as long as all of the general partners remain in the partnership. In general, what happens when a partner dies or leaves the partnership should be specified in the partnership agreement. If the partnership dissolves, the assets of the partnership are sold, the liabilities are settled, and the remainder distributed to the partners. The partnership agreement should state whether a partner can sell his or her share, under what conditions, and how the share of the assets and profits of the partnership will be determined. For example, does it require unanimous consent of the partners and will those profits be divided equally?

Taxes

The partnership itself incurs no taxes although it files a partnership tax return for informational purposes. Each partner pays personal taxes on his or her share of the business income. A partner may be required to pay taxes on income without having received any cash disbursal from the partnership. Investing in the professional advice of a lawyer or accountant is worthwhile.

Partnership Advantages	Partnership Disadvantages
Access to capital of more than one person	Mutual agency
Avoids double taxation	Unlimited personal liability
Access to skills, talents, and energy of more than one person	Cannot sell without consent of partners
Few legal formalities	Dissolves at death of partner

CORPORATION

The most complex business entity is the corporation. It is a separate legal entity that exists independently of its owners, referred to as stockholders, and may engage in business, make contracts, sue and be sued, own property, and pay taxes. The U.S. Supreme Court defines the corporation as "an artificial being, invisible, intangible, and existing only in contemplation of the law."[24]

---

24 Chief Justice John Marshall, cited by Roger L. Miller and Gaylord A. Jentz in *Business Law Today* (St. Paul, MN: West Publishing, 1994), p. 632.

Starting a Corporation

A corporation is the most complex of all the business entities to create. Once the owners decide to form a corporation, they must choose a state in which to incorporate. A corporation (also known as a "C corporation") accepts the regulations and restrictions of the state in which it is founded and any other state in which it chooses to do business. Most states require the owners to file Articles of Incorporation or a Certificate of Incorporation with the appropriate state office, again most commonly the secretary of state's office. In general, these articles include:

- The corporate name
- The number of shares of stock the corporation is authorized to issue
- The number of shares of stock each of the owners will buy
- Each owner's contribution to obtain these shares of stock
- The business of the corporation
- The management structure of the corporation (its directors and officers)

Although the assistance of an attorney may be valuable, most states allow businesses to incorporate without the assistance of an attorney, and some states even have "incorporation kits" to help in the process. There is a fee for filing the corporate documents and an annual fee for keeping the corporation in existence. States differ in the requirements they place on corporations. Delaware, for example, offers low incorporation fees, favorable laws, and minimal legal requirements, and many corporations are chartered there for these reasons. After approval from the secretary of state, the corporation pays its fees, and the approved articles of incorporation become its charter. The corporation then holds a stockholders meeting where the members formally elect a board of directors who will appoint the corporate officers.

Structure and Management

The corporation also needs ***bylaws***, the rules by which the corporation is run. Bylaws are general guidelines for managing a firm and specify such activities as annual stockholders meetings; meetings of the board of directors; and the number, titles, selection, and responsibilities of each officer. Because the corporate business entity is separate from its owners, it has to set up its own record-keeping system. The assets and liabilities, the profits and losses, are owned by the corporation and not by the shareholders.

Corporations may operate in states and countries in addition to the state in which they have incorporated. Corporations fall into three categories:

Domestic Corporation: operates in the state in which it was incorporated

Foreign Corporation: incorporated in one state but has operations in another, and therefore the other state considers it a *foreign corporation*

Alien Corporation: operates in a country in which it was not incorporated and so is considered an *alien corporation* in that country.

Management and Control

The owners, or the shareholders, of the corporation have to vote directly on certain major decisions, such as amendments to the articles of incorporation or dissolving the corporation. For most decision making that does not change the nature or character of the organization, the owners elect a group of individuals to act as the board of directors. Usually, each share of stock gets one vote. Those who hold a majority of the shares have ultimate control over the corporation. Shareholders can elect themselves to the board of directors.

The board of directors is responsible for providing guidance to the executive management team of the corporation. Directors may be paid for their services, although it is not required. The board of directors determines who fills the role of the key officers within the corporation, who, in turn, are responsible for running the day-to-day business.

If you own stock in a corporation, you may be paid a dividend, or cash distribution on the stock you own. A dividend must be paid equally to all shares of common stock and is usually expressed as an amount per share, such as "$5 per share." The board of directors typically decides whether dividends shall be paid, how much, and when.

Liability

Because a corporation is a separate legal entity, creditors of the corporation only have a claim against the assets of the corporation for payment. Individual shareholders are not personally liable for the losses of the business beyond their initial investment. This limited liability makes investment in a corporation very attractive and is a major advantage of the corporation form.

The Life and Sale of a Corporation

The corporation, as a separate legal entity, lasts as long as its shareholders decide it should. For practical purposes, a corporation's life is considered perpetual. It can be stated within its articles that a corporation will continue in ***perpetuity***. The sale of ownership rights in a corporation is through the sale of stock shares. Corporations can issue two types of stock: preferred and common.

9. ***Preferred stock*** conveys special ownership rights. The owners of this stock have a "preferred" claim on the profits of the company. This claim is in the form of a preferred dividend (if there is enough net income, the preferred stockholders are guaranteed a dividend). Preferred stockholders do not have a say in how the company is run and do not have voting rights in electing the board of directors.
10. ***Common stock*** conveys no special privileges with respect to the profits of the company but does convey voting rights in the corporation.

Shares of stock can be purchased from current owners (who wish to sell) or from the authorized and issued shares of the corporation. These transactions generally occur in the stock markets of the world.

Taxes and "Double Taxation"

As a separate legal entity, the corporation must file its own income tax returns and pay taxes on its profits. The corporation must report all income it has received from its business and may deduct certain IRS-approved expenses it has incurred while conducting its business. In addition to corporate income taxes, dividends paid to shareholders are regarded as personal income, and the shareholder must pay tax on that income. Therefore, corporations must pay these taxes at the *corporate* tax rate and then stockholders must pay taxes on the dividends they receive from these same profits at the *individual* tax rate. Thus, a corporation's profits are taxed twice. This ***double taxation*** is a distinct disadvantage of the corporate form of ownership. Legislation is now under review at the federal level that may change double taxation for corporations and not tax dividend earnings, therefore eliminating double taxation in the future.

C Corporation Advantages	C Corporation Disadvantages
Limited liability of owners	Costly to set up and maintain
Easy to transfer ownership to others	Double taxation
Easy to raise money and add additional owners	Legal and regulatory requirements
Ability to continue in perpetuity	Control of organization can be lost to larger shareholders

OTHER FORMS OF BUSINESS OWNERSHIP

With these three business entities in place—the sole proprietorship, partnership, and corporation—the Internal Revenue Service realized other forms of business were needed. Therefore, additional business entities have evolved over time and offer other entity options for business owners. Two of these options, the S Corporation and the Limited Liability Company, are presented here. You will notice that they combine select attributes of the partnership and the corporation business entities.

S CORPORATION

In 1954 the Internal Revenue Service Code created the "Sub-chapter Corporation" and subsequently shortened the title to "S Corporation" along with modifications in its qualifications. Although this is actually a special type of a partnership, an S Corporation is only a distinction for federal income tax purposes, and in terms of its legal characteristics, no different from any other corporation. If a corporation meets the S Corporation criteria, its shareholders must actually elect to be treated as one. All shareholders must consent to have the corporation treated as an S Corporation.[25]

S Corporation structure places limits on the type and number of shareholders and must meet the following requirements:

- The corporation has no more than 100 shareholders
- The corporation has only one class of stock
- All of the shareholders are U.S. residents, either citizens or resident aliens
- All of the shareholders are individuals (i.e., no corporations or other entities own the stock)
- The corporation operates on a calendar-year financial basis.

If the business satisfies these criteria, then the S Corporation is not liable for "double taxation." That is, the S Corporation does not pay taxes on the income generated by the business. Instead, the income or losses are passed through to the individual shareholders and reported on their tax returns. The income or losses are divided among the shareholders based upon the percentage of stock of the corporation that they own.

[25] Scarborough, Norman M., Doug Wilson, Thomas W. Zimmerer, *Essentials of Entrepreneurship and Small Business Management,* 5th ed. (Upper Saddle River, NJ: Pearson Education, 2008), p. 179.

S Corporation Advantages	S Corporation Disadvantages
Limited liability of owners	One hundred shareholder limit
Avoids double taxation	Some legal and regulatory requirements
Ability to continue in perpetuity	Shareholders can only be individuals
Easy to transfer ownership to others	Control of organization can be lost to larger shareholders

LIMITED LIABILITY COMPANY

The newest business entity recognized by the IRS is a Limited Liability Company, or LLC. This is another "hybrid" form of business and was introduced in part as a response to our litigious business climate. An LLC offers the simplicity of a partnership with the legal protection of a corporation.

Like S Corporations, LLCs offer their owners limited personal liability for the debts of the business and, therefore, provide a significant advantage over sole proprietorships and partnerships. LLCs, however, are not subject to many of the restrictions currently imposed on S Corporations and offer additional flexibility compared to S Corporations. An LLC is created according to the laws of the state where the business is located and in most states, an LLC can have multiple owners, with a few states requiring LLCs to have at least two owners. LLC owners are referred to as "members" and may include non-U.S. citizens, partnerships, and corporations. An LLC does not restrict its members' ability to become involved in managing the company. These advantages make the LLC an attractive form of ownership for many companies, and due to these benefits LLCs have become a popular form of business ownership.[26]

Starting an LLC

Creating an LLC is similar to creating a corporation. It requires the owners to create two documents: the articles of organization (which must be filed with the secretary of state) and the operating agreement. The LLC's articles of organization establish its name, address, method of management (board-managed or member-managed), duration, and the names and addresses of each owner. Unlike a corporation, an LLC does not have perpetual life and in most states, an LLC's charter may not exceed 30 years. The operating agreement, similar to a corporation's bylaws, outlines the provisions governing the way the LLC will conduct business, such as its members' capital contributions to the LLC, the admission or withdrawal of members, distributions from the business, and how the LLC will be managed.[27]

LLC Considerations

Despite their appeal, LLCs do have disadvantages. They can be expensive to create, they have limited life spans, are not suitable for companies whose owners plan to raise money through an initial public offering or who want to use stock options or an employee stock ownership plan as incentives for employees. Owners who want to provide attractive benefits to themselves and their employees will not find this form of ownership appealing because the cost of those benefits is not tax deductible in an LLC.

---

[26] Scarborough, Norman M., Doug Wilson, and Thomas W. Zimmerer *Essentials of Entrepreneurship and Small Business Management*, 5th ed. (Upper Saddle River, NJ: Pearson Education, 2008), p. 181.
[27] Ibid., p. 182.

LLC Advantages	LLC Disadvantages
Limited personal liability	Cannot sell without consent of partners
Does not require strict government reporting	Control of organization can be lost to larger shareholders
Avoids double taxation	Limited life and dissolves at death of partner

Selecting the "Right" Form Of Business

No single form of business ownership is ideal for all. When two or more owners are involved, a sole proprietorship is not a fit, and they need to look at other suitable options. If there are "risk" concerns regarding the nature of the business, then an LLC or corporation may be the best choices to consider. An attorney and a CPA are good advisors to consult with regarding selecting the best business entity.

Review and Discussion Questions

1. What are the advantages and disadvantages of a sole proprietorship, a partnership, an LLC, and a corporation?

2. What is the relationship between a common stockholder and the board of directors?

3. Which of the business organizations restricts the number of owners?

4. Which organization offers the optimal situation for raising capital?

5. What might be the best choice for a single business owner that is starting up a small "experimental" venture? Why might that choice be attractive?

6. What do the articles of partnership include?

7. What are the similarities and differences between an S Corporation and an LLC?

8. What are the benefits of an LLC versus a partnership or a corporation? Why would an organization choose one over the others?

9. Pressure has been placed on the federal government to change the tax laws for corporations so double taxation no longer applies. How might that change the value of owning stock?

Chapter **9**

Developing a Business Plan

The value is not in the document itself, but in what you learn as you create it.

Key terms to look for:

- Executive summary
- Mission statement
- Pro forma statements
- SWOT analysis
- Vision statement

To create sound business decisions, you must first have a cohesive plan that supports clearly defined success measurements. Your product positioning, marketing, production, and finance plans should all align strategically in support of your objective.

A business plan is a written summary of a proposed or existing business venture, its operational and financial details, its marketing opportunities and strategy, and its managers' skills and abilities. The value in creating a business plan is not just the creation of the document but also the benefits that come from the process of researching and thinking about your business in a more structured and thorough manner. Planning also helps to look at your ideas critically. It requires an investment of time and may help to avoid costly and perhaps disastrous mistakes later.

The Purpose of the Business Plan

Fundamentally, a business plan allows you to create more objectivity around a business idea by looking at it holistically for problems and pitfalls. More importantly, this objectivity provides an opportunity to find innovative solutions. A successful business plan effectively communicates the market need, the product and/or service solution, projected profitability, and who you are and why you believe you can make it work. A business plan serves three essential functions:

1. To guide owners and their strategic and operational planning
2. To attract potential lenders and investors
3. To substantiate the potential for success of the venture.

Content and Structure

While the basic elements of a business plan may be somewhat standard, there is no single "correct" outline for a business plan. The plan must fit the particular business, the circumstances, and the intended audience. The manner in which owners "tell their business story" is intended to be unique. For example, a business plan designed to inform employees of the company's long-term strategic intents may be promulgated differently from one intended to appeal to bank lenders and venture capitalists. Ideally, the business plan serves as a map to better guide the direction of a proposed or existing business venture. Regardless of format, there are common major process phases to business planning:

- Establishing a strategic vision for the company *(making sure it aligns with your success measurements)*
- Determining the current state of the industry and the market *(situation analysis)*
- Completing a SWOT analysis on the organization *(internal strengths and weaknesses and external opportunities and threats)*
- Determining the specific tactics within each of the company's functional elements that you believe will best support the strategic vision*(research and development, marketing, production, and finance)*
- Monitoring progress by establishing benchmarks and conducting competitor analysis comparisons *(how will success and failure be monitored and assessed?)*

Business Plan Outline

The following is a general outline of what most business plans contain:

I. Executive Summary

II. Mission Statement (and possibly a vision statement)

IV. Objectives

V. Company Description/Profile

VI. Product and/or Service Description

VII. Market and Customer Analysis

VIII. Strategy and Implementation

IX. Management and Organizational Structure

X. Financial Plan

XI. Appendices

> **In Foundation™**
>
> Business planning is the process of developing a strategic vision for the organization. In Foundation™, all teams start with an identical profile. Your company has a history, but no specific business philosophy. Your job is to determine the future nature of your organization. Describe where you want the business to go and how you intend to get it there. There is no "magic bullet" strategy in Foundation. Successful teams will develop a cogent long-range plan, align their internal functions in support of the plan, and adjust as dictated by the opportunities and realities of the marketplace. The business plan can also be used as a strategic planning tool and a vehicle to communicate the status of the business to new owners and managers.

Executive Summary

The executive summary provides a brief overview of the plan that lies ahead. It captures key highlights in an orderly manner that describes the venture and creates interest for the reader to proceed. It is a miniature business plan that should convey:

1. The business concept (solution)
2. Market (need)
3. How you plan to meet it (profitability)
4. Make key assertions

The executive summary is the opportunity to make a bold statement, without providing the justification contained in the more detailed plan. Conversely, the executive summary is not merely an abstract of the business plan, an introduction to the business plan, a preface or a random collection of highlights. Remember, everything you state in the executive summary must be supported and proved in the rest of the plan.

Mission Statement
An organization's mission is its reason for existing. A mission statement describes the business in terms of goods, markets, services, and client needs. The mission statement should define an organization's ultimate strategic intent for profitability, growth, market share, and building competitive advantage. The mission statement should be a concise statement of business strategy and answer three questions:

1. What do we do?
2. How do we do it?
3. For whom do we do it?

Vision Statement
A vision statement is a relatively new addition to the business plan. The vision statement describes goals at a high level that coincide with the owner's business goals. The vision should state what the owners envision the business to become in terms of its growth, values, employees, and contributions to society. As a complement to the mission statement, the vision statement sets the stage to develop strategies for moving the organization toward that vision. Remember, your vision and mission statements are meant to help guide the business, not to limit your direction. As your company evolves and the competitive environment changes, your mission and vision for the business need to adapt. Therefore, your vision and mission statements should be periodically revisited and revised as needed.

Objectives
The objectives of your plan describe specific goals that are quantifiable and measurable. These objectives provide focus toward what your business intends to accomplish. The implementation of your plan depends on being able to track progress and measure your results based on these stated objectives.

Company Description/Profile
In one or two brief paragraphs, summarize this information:

- Nature of your company
- Market need you are meeting
- How you plan to meet the need
- Distinctive competencies you have or will gain

Product and/or Service Description
Provide a clear description of how your customer will view and handle your product. Pictures and diagrams save words and keep your plan interesting. Items like product specification sheets are best put into the appendices. The plan should answer these questions:

- What are the expected life-cycles?
- What are potential add-on or next generation products?
- What intellectual protection (patents, trademarks, etc.) exist?
- What are the planned areas of research and development?
- How does your solution compare to your competitors'?

Market and Customer Analysis

Although your product or service will determine industry competitors and customers, the Market Analysis should be focused on the market and the conditions, not on your solution. Clearly establishing the market sets the background for the solution.

Industry Analysis - This section demonstrates an understanding of direct competitors, including substitutes for your product or service. If you are entering a new or expanding market niche, which competitors are likely to enter? The number, size, and history of the competitors will drive your strategy for entry and growth. Identify your key competitors (or groups), their current share in the market, and how important the market is to them. Useful tools for characterizing the degree of competitiveness in the market are SWOT, TOWS and Porter's Five Forces analyses. This type of information can concisely be presented in tables. Noting key competitors is important, but extensive data belongs in an appendix.

Key parameters of an industry analysis include:

- Number of competitors
- Nature of competitors
- Growth of the market
- Major customer groups

Market Segmentation and Target Market - Who will be buying your product? Will you distribute to businesses in a business-to-business (B2B) arrangement, or to consumers in a business-to-consumer (B2C) arrangement? The nature of your customer will drive marketing and sales efforts. Clearly describe the unmet need you will be solving. The remainder of the plan should describe how you can meet this need better than anyone else based upon:

- Distinguishing characteristics
- Primary target market size
- Expected market penetration (share)
- Pricing, margins, and expected discounts (or rebates)
- How you will identify your target market
- Marketing media
- Customer purchasing cycle
- Secondary market attributes (why are they *secondary* market?)

Strategy and Implementation
This section summarizes your key strategies for the venture. This may involve plans that relate to funding, getting the right people involved, and marketing. For example, you may choose to describe your strategies for making your target customer aware of your product and how you will accomplish the following:

- Market penetration
- Growth
- Distribution
- Communication
- Sales force
- Sales activities

Timeline or Milestones
A clear timeline with milestones demonstrates that you understand the requirements (and hurdles) for succeeding. These milestones should correspond with who will be responsible, start and end dates, and the funds required for each task.

Operations
Operations are often left out or overemphasized. Show you have a clear understanding of how your product or service will be produced, without going through all of the details. The strategy for operations must be congruent with your market. A differentiated production strategy in a low-cost market will quickly be dismissed. If you are in the early stages of development, explain the criteria you must meet to be successful.

Management and Organizational Structure
Key elements of any business are the character and drive of management, how the company is structured, and who owns it. The management team and advisors are the foundation of all successful businesses. Leadership, innovation, and determination can make or break a business. The management and advisory teams establish your credibility.

Management Team
Include a brief description of your key players and their roles. Just as important, identify the skills and experience you are missing and how and when you plan to fill them. The timing of additions to the management team should match with growth expectations. A chart of your management structure is an excellent way to show relationships.

Board of Advisors
The best source of information and advice is from people who are already in the industry you plan to enter, have had experience in their own business, or have experience serving your competitors. People who have established their own businesses will be able to quickly identify problems with your plan and solution. Do not just list these individuals, *use* them. Surround yourself with people who are experienced where you are weak. The plan should reflect their input, so keep your description concise. Be sure to include the advisors' names with a brief background and the area of expertise they provide. As a company matures, these individuals may become part of a board of trustees. With a more formal board, position titles and past contributions also become essential information.

Financial Plan
The financial plan section should convey information in these areas:

- Current funding needs
- How (or for what) they will be used
- The projected financial status of the business
- Expected return for the investor (loan, equity, equity or convertible debt)

Investors are compensated by the level of risk they take. The last part of funding requirements is relaying the strategies for exiting or repaying your investors.

For existing business ventures, the financial plan has two parts, historic and future. Operational businesses should have a clear financial history. This section establishes your fiscal credibility. The financial plan also presents cash flow projections for the first 12 months of your business. Do you have enough working capital to cover negative months? What do years two and three look like? Cash flow is a critical part of any business plan.

Pro forma (or future) financial projects should be an objective assessment that includes all of the milestones and strategies you have outlined in your plan. Every change that involves revenues or expenses in your business plan should be reflected in your financials.

Obtaining funding requires establishing the value of your business and the value the funding will provide. Four things that determine the value are:

1. Amount of capital already invested
2. Intellectual protection
3. Value of assets held
4. Business potential

Your business plan's financial section often includes or is followed by the following information:

- General financial assumptions
- Break-even analysis
- Profit-and-loss statement
- Cash-flow statement
- Balance sheet
- Comparative business ratios

Images, Tables and Charts
Most business plans benefit from the use of images, tables, and charts integrated into its text to better tell the business story. Illustrating concepts and numbers through tables and charts relating to the sales forecast, the profit-and-loss statement, and the cash-flow statement can be valuable communication tools. For example, a photo of a target market customer using the product, a pie chart showing market share, and bar graphs illustrating monthly cash-flow projections can be powerful.

Appendices

"Should this information be in the plan?" If that is a question you find yourself asking, it may be better to include it in an appendix. Review the appendices to make sure that these additions support your plan and are referred to in the body of the plan itself. If not, you may want to keep the information for your own reference, but take it out of the plan. The following, in an order that flows with your plan, may be possible considerations for the appendices:[23]

- Market studies
- Patents
- Pertinent published information
- Pictures of products
- Pro forma financial statements
- Professional references
- Resumes of key managers
- Significant contracts

> **In Foundation - Your Business Plan**
>
> The business plan that you develop will have to be appropriate to the current situation of your company. It will give the reader a sense of what your business is about.
>
> To create a business plan for your Foundation company, you need to:
> - *Develop or state your strategy and mission statement.*
> - *Outline your company's marketing, production, and financial plans and actions.*
> - *Describe your current condition – good or bad – to communicate key facts about your business.*
> - *Translate that information into a cohesive document that "tells the story" of your business.*
> - *Create an executive summary that engages the reader and makes him or her want to learn more about your business.*

Altitude and Audience

Altitude is the respective level at which you research and write your plan and determines the level of detail needed. Your research should be as "close to the ground" as possible. The plan should be written at an altitude that allows readers to quickly grasp your plan without losing the innovative aspects of the solution. One challenge is keeping your altitude consistent and at an elevation that gives readers enough information but does not overwhelm or distract them. Knowing your audience helps. Normally your audience is educated but unfamiliar with your business. Avoid abbreviations, jargon, and trade slang, both from your industry and from your business.

[23] *Outline for a Business Plan: A Proven Approach for Entrepreneurs Only*, Ernst & Young LLP, 1997.

Business Plan Resources
Many resources are available to assist with creating business plans. This includes numerous books, workbooks, software programs, Web sites, professional business consultants, and government-sponsored organizations such as the Small Business Administration and SCORE.

For a list of Small Business Development Center (SBDC) locations, see the Small Business Administration's SBDC Web page at http://www.sba.gov/SBDC.

Marketing, Operational, and Financial Aspects of Your Foundation Business Plan

The marketing section of your Foundation business plan will seek to address these questions:

- *Will you price above, at, or below industry averages?*
- *If you are going to price high, how will you justify those prices?*
- *If you select a low price strategy, how will you keep margins large enough to result in a profit?*
- *Will your pricing strategies be different for each market segment?*
- *How much will you spend on advertising and sales?*
- *What do you hope to achieve with your advertising expenditures?*
- *Are you a cost-conscious company, or are you willing to spend whatever is necessary to be well known by every potential customer?*

The operations and production section of your business plan will answer these questions:

- *Will you be better off investing in automation, capacity, or both?*
- *Will you keep overtime to a minimum, or will you run a lot of overtime as an alternative to capacity expansions?*
- *Which of the factories will you liquidate, if any, and how?*

The financial section of your business plan will want to discuss responses to these questions:

- *What is your strategy for raising capital and managing debt?*
- *What are your ownership and stock and dividend policies?*
- *Will you raise capital through short-term debt, long-term debt, stock issues, liquidate factory resources, or a combination of these means?*
- *How will you manage and maintain cash reserves to avoid high-interest emergency loans?*

FOUNDATION BUSINESS STRATEGIES

The following strategies may be consideration for your Foundation business planning:

Overall Cost Leader

An overall cost leader will attempt to be the low-cost producer in both segments of the market. It will have good profit margins on all sales while keeping prices low for price-sensitive customers.

Firm Profile:

- More likely to reposition products than introduce new ones to the market
- Capacity improvements are unlikely to be undertaken (may run overtime instead)
- Automation may be pursued to increase margins
- Investments will be financed with debt and/or stock issues
- Tends to spend less on promotion and sales
- Focuses on Market Share, Profits, and Stock Price

Cost Leader with Low-Tech Focus

A low-tech focused cost leader seeks to dominate the price sensitive market segments. Its aim is to set prices below all competitors—and still be profitable.

Firm Profile:

- Multiple product lines in the low-tech segment
- Invests heavily in automation
- Spends moderately on advertising to cost-sensitive customers (sales people have more than one product to pitch to prospects)
- Investments financed with debt and/or stock issues
- Focuses on ROS, ROE, and profits

Cost Leader with a Product Life-Cycle Focus

A product life-cycle focused cost leader will seek to minimize costs through efficiency and expertise. Products will be allowed to age and change in appeal from high-tech to low-tech buyers.

Firm Profile:

- Low R&D spending (very little repositioning & new product every two to three years)
- Invests in automation early in the product's life-cycle
- Moderate spending on promotion and sales
- Focuses on ROE, ROS, and profits

Differentiation

A differentiator will seek to create maximum awareness and brand equity. It wants to be well known as a maker of high quality/highly desirable products.

Firm Profile:

- High R&D spending to keep products fresh
- Maintains a presence in both market segments
- Spends heavily on advertising and sales to create maximum awareness and accessibility
- Prices tend to be higher
- Focuses on market share, profits, and stock price

Differentiator with High-Tech Focus

A high-tech differentiator seeks to be known far and wide as the top producer of the best performing state-of-the-art products.

Firm Profile:

- Multiple product lines in the high-tech segment
- Minimum focus in the other segment
- High promotion and sales investments to create optimal awareness and accessibility
- High R&D expenditures to continually introduce new product lines and keep existing products fresh
- Unlikely to invest in increased automation or production capacity
- Focuses on ROA, asset turnover, and ROE

Differentiator with a Product Life-Cycle Focus

A product life-cycle differentiator seeks to be well known as a top producer of good-performing products in each of the targeted segments.

Firm Profile:

- Multiple product lines in both segments
- High promotion and sales investments to create maximum awareness and accessibility
- High R&D expenditures to continually reposition product lines to keep them fresh
- Unlikely to invest in increased automation or production capacity
- Focus on ROA, stock price, and asset turnover

Glossary

An online business glossary that you may find useful is:
http://www.nytimes.com/library/financial/glossary/bfglosa.htm

A

Accessibility The availability of the product for the customer to gain access to. The higher the accessibility, the more easily a customer may purchase a particular team's product. Investments in the distribution network improve a product's accessibility.

Accounting A summary and analysis of the firm's financial position.

Accounts Payable Amount owed to suppliers for raw materials delivered. This value is affected by the number of days taken to pay suppliers (Accounts Payable expressed in days) which may be adjusted on the marketing screen.

Accounts Receivable The amount of money owed to the company by its debtors. This value is affected by both sales volume and credit policy (accounts receivable lag, expressed in days).

Accumulated Depreciation
Cumulative total of each year's depreciation charge for plant and equipment.

Actual Industry Unit Sales
Units actually sold into the segment from all products represented. If this value is lower than Available Unit Sales then insufficient units were produced for sale into the segment.

Adjustment for Non-cash Items
Adjustments for income statement transactions, where no cash actually changed hands.

Administration Cost of general administration such as legal services, accounting, and human resources.

Age The preferred perceived age customers would like a product to possess. Perceived age is affected by redesigning the product (changing the performance attribute, size attribute, or both).

Assets Anything owned by a firm—the organization's "stuff."

Asset Turnover Sales, generated in a particular year, divided by the value of total assets for the same period.

Automation The automation the company will enjoy on each of its production lines during the coming round.

B

Balance Sheet Reports the book value of all assets, liabilities, and owner's equity of the firm at a point in time.

Benchmarking A method of evaluating the performance of a business by comparison to some other specified level of accomplishment, typically a level achieved by another company.

Benefits The annual cost of the benefits package for each employee.

Board of Directors A set of executives who are responsible for monitoring the activities of the firm's president and other high-level managers, also referred to as the executive management team.

Book Value The amount an asset is valued at in business records; not necessarily the same amount as what the asset is worth on the open market.

Bonds Long-term debt securities purchased by investors.

Business Plan A detailed description of a proposed or existing business including the product or services offered, the types of customers it would attract, the competition, and the facilities needed for production.

C

Capacity The straight-time capacity the company will enjoy, on each of its production lines, during the coming round.

Cash The amount of cash in the bank.

Cash-Flow Statement This statement is published in conformity with the Finance and Accounting Standards Board's (FASB) most recent statements and opinions on the format for a cash-flow analysis.

Cash from Long-Term Debt
Cash received for issuing new, ten-year bonds is an example of cash generated from long-term debt.

Change in Current Assets and Liabilities
Items in this category are assets and liabilities that have either increased or decreased since last year's balance sheet. As such, the line items either expel or draw in cash.

Change in Current Debt
This is the net value of any current debt owed (and therefore had to be paid) last year and any additional current debt acquired.

Close The price being paid for the bond in the third-party market at the end of the last period. This price is a function of the interest rate and the risk inherent in the security as expressed by its credit rating.

Closing Cash Position Value in the cash account at the end of this year, also shown on the Balance Sheet.

Common Stock Value of monies received for the issuing of stock since the company's inception (the value of additional paid-in capital is included here).

Contribution Margin Sales revenue less all of the variable costs (does not include depreciation).

Cumulative Profits Cumulative total of all profits (losses) generated since the game's inception.

Current Debt The value of debt owed and payable on January 1st of the year for which decisions are currently being made.

Customer Awareness That portion of the total segment that was aware of a particular segment.

Customer Survey This is an assessment of the desirability of a particular product

D

Depreciation An accounting for the portion of the equipment that was effectively "used up" in the period. The government recognizes this wear and tear and allows it to be deducted before declaring a profit. It is added back to get a true picture of the cash account. Although depreciation is expensed on the income statement, no company check was actually written. Unlike a check for the rent, the cash account never saw a check for depreciation.

Direct Labor Cost of all labor associated with manufacturing the product. This value may be impacted by raising or lowering the amount of automation (a capital cost) present on a particular line.

Direct Material Cost of all raw materials necessary to manufacture a product.

Dividends The income the firm provides to its owners, or shareholders, based on profits.

Dividends Paid Value of cash expended on paying dividends. Dividend payment is made on the finance screen and each year defaults to zero unless another value is entered.

E

Earnings Before Interest and Taxes (EBIT)
Net margin less fees, write-offs, and bonus income; this information appears on the income statement.

Earnings per Share (EPS)
EPS is calculated by dividing net profit into the number of shares outstanding.

Economies of Scale The process where the cost of each good produced decreases as the volume produced increases. This reduction in cost per unit occurs when the initial investment of capital is shared with an increasing number of units of output, and therefore, the cost of producing a good or service decreases as production increases.

Emergency Loan Amount of cash injected during the year when the company is completely devoid of cash. This is usually a result of inventories building at unexpected levels thus drying up all liquidity. Loans made on an emergency basis have a punitive interest rate (5% above current rate) attached to them.

F

Face Value The face value of the entire bond issue. This value is also what would be paid back to the bondholders at the maturity of the debt. However, if bonds are retired (called in) early the amount paid may be higher or lower than this.

Fees and Write-offs This is a compilation of charges that may be incurred during any given period.

G

Gain/Loss on Equipment Sales
If machinery is sold at a value that is higher than the net or depreciated value of the machinery, then this shows up as a profit on the income statement. Such gains and losses must be reported on the income statement. However they do not represent a true movement of cash. The cash flow is the total amount received for selling off the line, this amount is shown (net of any purchases) in the cash flows from the investing section of the cash-flow statement.

Gross Margin Revenue left after deducting direct labor, raw materials, and depreciation expressed as a percentage of sales.

Growth Rate Annual compound rate at which unit demand will grow.

I

Income Statement The income statement, also known as a profit-and-loss statement, shows the entire value that an account has accumulated over the previous period (in this case twelve months).

Industry Sales Dollar sales into each segment.

Industry Unit Sales Total units sold by all companies into each segment.

Industry Unit Sales vs. Unit Demand
The number of units sold, by all companies, in each segment of the market, versus the number of units demanded. In cases where the units demanded is larger than the units sold, there was an inadequate supply of minimally acceptable product available and thus some demand was unfulfilled.

Inventory Carrying Costs
The cost of having inventory in stock.

Inventory Turnover The relationship between the cost of goods sold and inventory calculated by cost of goods sold/inventory.

Inventory Value The value of inventory on hand valued using "average cost accounting." This will rise and fall based on the production scheduled (on the production screen) versus units sold.

L

Labor Cost — The per-unit cost of labor in the year just ended.

Leverage — Total assets at the end of the period under review divided by owners' equity for the same period.

List Price — Price charged for the product in the round just ended.

Long-Term Debt — The value of all outstanding bonds (ten-year) that will become due at some future date.

Long-Term Interest — Interest paid on outstanding bonds.

M

Market Share — Overall percentage share, of the dollar volume, gained each year.

Market Share Actual — Market share actually achieved by each product in each segment of the market. The market shares based on units are shown in the left-hand group of columns and the market shares based on dollars are shown in the right-hand group of columns.

Market Share Actual vs. Potential — Compares what was sold by a team into a segment with what the team would have sold if they had produced sufficient inventory.

Market Share by Segment — Dollar market share of each segment enjoyed by each team.

Market Share Potential — This shows the respective market shares each product should have earned if all products had been manufactured in sufficient quantity. In cases where actual share is larger than potential share, then other teams ran out of product and "chased" demand to a team with an inferior product. In cases where potential share is larger than actual, then the team stocked out and chased demand to other teams.

Material Cost — The per-unit cost of direct materials in the year just ended.

Mean Time Between Failure — Also referred to as MTBF, this measures the reliability of product expressed in a standard unit of measure, such as in thousands of hours. It is the average time between expected product failures. The longer the duration, or MTBF, the better the product performs.

N

Net Cash from Operations

The subtotal of all activities on the cash-flow statement to this point. Conceptually it is the actual cash either generated (if positive) or used up (if negative) by the core activities of the business. The remainder of the cash-flow statement summarizes activities involved in either capital budgeting or tax and treasury activities.

Net Change in Cash Position

The difference between the balance in the cash account at the end of last year and the value of cash account at the end of this year. The entire cash-flow statement is designed to reconcile to this value.

Net Income Value of profits as calculated on the income statement.

Net Margin Value of total sales less variable and period costs.

Net Profit Earnings left after all expenses are paid. Net profit can only be allocated to one of two directions: It is either paid out to the owners of the business in the form of dividends, or it is retained in the business to grow the company and is thus added to the Retained Earnings of the business.

O

Overtime Typically paid at 1.5 times the expected wage, this can also be expressed as the percentage of the production that was undertaken using overtime.

P

Percent of Market Share of total units sold, represented by each segment of the market.

Perceptual Map A graph showing marketing information, such as a particular segment of the market and identifies all products that sold 1% or more into that segment.

Period Costs Costs that generally tend not to move in proportion to sales volume.

Plant Utilization Volume actually produced during the previous round compared to the actual capacity for that round. For example, levels in excess of 100% indicate overtime was utilized.

Plant and Equipment Gross value of capacity and automation available (or purchased) for each production line.

Plant Improvements Net value, after deducting any equipment sold for scrap, of cash invested in automation and capacity.

Positioning Proximity of product to the "sweet spot" within the segment.

Price Price charged for a product this year.

Price/Earnings Ratio

The closing stock price divided by the earnings per share or EPS. The P/E is sometimes referred to as the earnings multiple, or simply, the multiple.

Primary Segment The segment into which the largest proportion of this product was sold.

Production vs. Capacity
Number of units actually built versus the straight-time capacity of the entire plant for the year just ended. When production is larger than capacity, overtime must have been scheduled in order to achieve the production level.

Profits This shows the dollar profit earned each year since the game's inception.

Profit Sharing That share or percentage of the profits paid to technicians and assemblers as per the union agreement.

Promotions Budget Value of monies expended on media advertising, as set on the Marketing screen.

Q

Quality Desired performance standard of a product or service. This may be measured by MTBF of the product.

R

R&D Costs Annual costs associated with redesigning an existing, or designing an entirely new, product. If an R&D project is more than a year in duration, then the cost will be charged out over the full life of the project, with a maximum of 1 million dollars being charged on a single project in any given year. For example, if a project is estimated to cost $1.5 million then $1 million will be charged against this year's income statement and $.5 million will be charged against the next year's.

Retained Earnings Total of all company profits and losses of the life of the company, less any dividends paid out. This *does not* represent a pile of cash. The monies are captured in the assets of the company. This may be cash, but it may just as easily be in the form of plant/equipment or even accounts receivable.

Retirement of Long-Term Debt
Cash consumed in the early retirement of bonds that are outstanding. These bonds are retired at the value at which they were trading in the third party market at the end of the previous year.

Revision Date The last time product came out of a redesign cycle, in R&D, or the next time it will come out of the redesign cycle if it is currently being redesigned.

ROA Return on Assets; net profit divided by the value of total assets for the same period.

ROE Return on Equity; net profit divided by the value of owners' equity for that year.

ROS Return on sales; net profit divided by total sales for the same period.

S

S&P The Standard and Poor's credit rating for additional underwriting of debt for the company; it ranges from AAA to D.

Sales The value of products sold over the previous twelve months, broken out by product line.

Sales Budget Monies expended for paying sales personnel and expanding the distribution network. This value is an input on the Marketing screen.

Sales of Common Stock Value of cash received from the issuing of additional stock. Maximum issue in any year is 20% of the total currently outstanding stock. Stock is issued at its spot prices as of December 31st of the year just ended.

Series Number The first half of a bond issue's series number refers to the interest or coupon rate paid on the bonds, which are issued in $1000 denominations. The second half of the series number (after the letter "S" which is placed there by convention) refers to the date of maturity, for example a "10" after the "S" would indicate the bond is to mature in the year 2010.

SG&A % Sales Total of selling general and administrative expenses as a percentage of total sales for that period.

Shares Number of shares currently outstanding. At the beginning of the game each company has 2 million shares outstanding.

Short-Term Interest Interest paid on current debt, including interest on emergency loans.

Stock Out A situation where all products are sold out and it has had a negative effect on sales performance. Thus, it is likely a higher sales level would have been experienced had more units been manufactured and available.

T

Taxes Taxes paid on income, using a 35% taxation rate.

Total Assets Total of all current and fixed assets.

Total Equity Also known as shareholder equity, owners' equity, or net worth. This represents the net value of the company after liabilities are deducted from the value of total assets. The value is calculated by adding, in this case, common stock and retained earnings. This highlights the inherent relationship of the balance sheet. This relationship being owners' equity equals total assets less total liabilities.

Total Fixed Assets The value of plant and equipment less total accumulated depreciation.

Total Liabilities Sum total of accounts payable, current debt, and long-term debt.

Total Period Costs Accumulation of all period costs described above.

Total Units Demanded Total units that could have been sold into each segment had sufficient, appropriate product been made available.

U

Units in Inventory Number of units of the product left in inventory as of December 31st (in thousands of units).

Unit Sales vs. Unit Demand
Number of units our company sold, in each segment of the market, versus the number of units that segment wished to purchase from our company. In cases where the units demanded is greater than units sold, we did not build sufficient product and thus stocked out. In cases where units demanded are less than units sold, other teams stocked out and pushed demand to us that our product did not "deserve." However, as our product was minimally acceptable, it was begrudgingly purchased by the market.

Units' Sold The total number of this product sold into all market segments.

V

Variable Costs Costs that vary in direct proportion to the number of units sold.

W

Wage Escalator Annual cost of living adjustment applied to assemblers and technicians' hourly wages.

Y

Yield Dividend payment as a percentage value of the closing stock price, or the interest paid on the bond divided by the actual trading price of the bond.

Index

O

P

Q

R

S

T

U

V

W

Y

Breinigsville, PA USA
03 August 2010
242898BV00003B/5/P